A SEASON ON THE RESERVATION

ALSO BY KAREEM ABDUL–JABBAR

Black Profiles in Courage

Giant Steps

Kareem

A SEASON ON THE RESERVATION

MY SOJOURN WITH
THE WHITE MOUNTAIN APACHE

KAREEM ABDUL-JABBAR

with Stephen Singular

WILLIAM MORROW AND COMPANY, INC. ■ NEW YORK

Library of Congress Cataloging-in-Publication Data

Abdul-Jabbar, Kareem, 1947–

A season on the reservation: my soujourn with the White Mountain Apache / Kareem Abdul-Jabbar and Stephen Singular. — 1st. ed.

p.   cm.

ISBN 0-688-17077-3

1. Abdul-Jabbar, Kareem, 1947–   2. Basketball—Coaching.

3. White Mountain Apache Indians—Arizona.

I. Singular, Stephen.

II. Title.

GV884.A24A33   2000

796.323'092—dc21

[B]   99-27743

CIP

Printed in the United States of America

First Edition

1   2   3   4   5   6   7   8   9   10

BOOK DESIGN BY CARLA BOLTE

www.williammorrow.com

This book is dedicated to my family with thanks for their inspiration and love. My parents, especially my mom, Cora, are at the top of the list but I would be remiss if I failed to mention my children Habiba, Kareem, Sultana, Amir, and Adam. Finally I wish to acknowledge and thank that super family, the White Mountain Apache Tribe. Particular thanks go to the Eagle Clan who welcomed me to their homes and shared with me their knowledge of the way.

America is a country of many races and faces. This is my journal of my stay with some of my fellow Americans. In sharing it, I hope to increase the understanding of who we are for *all* Americans.

A SEASON ON THE RESERVATION

OKAY, GENTLEMEN!" RUSTY TAYLOR SAID TO the group of boys gathered in the weight room at the Alchesay High School gymnasium in Whiteriver, Arizona. They'd come together on this early November afternoon for the opening practice of the 1998–99 basketball season. Taylor paced in front of them in short, aggressive strides and barked out his words:

"Now listen up, men! First of all—no rattails!"

Sixty teenagers were scattered throughout the weight room, some sitting on the cement floor, others leaning against the scuffed walls or the big iron weight machines. They had the slovenly appearance—worn tennis shoes, cutoff sweatshirts, old basketball shorts—and the cocky attitude of young athletes everywhere. They had come to the weight room to try out for the Alchesay Falcons, but many of them now glared at Taylor and gave out a collective groan.

"Oh, man," one said with defiance in his voice. "No tails?"

"No rattails," Taylor repeated.

He reached around and touched the nape of his neck, making a snipping motion with his fingers. The nape was where White Mountain Apache boys liked to grow out the strands of hair that signaled a fashion statement on the reservation. Rattails were definitely cool at Alchesay High, and a number of the kids in the weight room were sporting them.

"They have to go," Taylor said. "Understand? I have no rattail and Coach Mendoza has no rattail and Mr. Jabbar has no . . ."

He glanced over at my bald head.

"Hair," I said from the corner, putting my hand on my clean scalp to make the point.

The room exploded with laughter. The kids looked up at me and smiled for the first time. Until now, they'd stared at me as if they didn't know what to think about this older and taller stranger in their midst, someone they'd heard of but didn't really know anything about.

The ice had been cracked and this was a good beginning, just what I'd been hoping for. I had never coached anywhere before and hadn't been around high school kids for several decades. When I'd arrived at the reservation three days earlier, I hadn't known what to expect. I was still feeling my way.

I wanted the kids to be comfortable with me, to know that I wasn't an intimidating outsider or just a casual visitor to their world. Sports celebrities occasionally came to the reservation, but only to spend a few days and a lot of money shooting the big game that lived in the 800,000 acres of ponderosa pine forest around Whiteriver. Those athletic stars quickly bagged an elk, a deer, or a bear and then left the area, barely speaking to the locals.

I was going to be living right next to the reservation and coaching at Alchesay for the next four months. I wanted the kids to know that I was not just passing through, and that I was not all that different from them, just older. I'd once been a teenager, too, a minority just as they are, a tall and awkward young man who'd struggled with all the doubts and insecurities they were now dealing with. I'd feared my coaches and had never wanted to be embarrassed in front of my peers. I'd wondered what the adult world was like and thought a lot about the mysteries of love and sex that lay ahead. I'd since raised sons of my own and lived with them through their own teenage trials.

The laughter had quieted down, so Taylor continued laying down the team rules.

"No more hickeys on your necks, gentlemen," he said. "You tell your girlfriends, 'Thank you, but no thank you.' It's just not right, and we don't want to see any more hickeys. Are we clear on this?"

More groans echoed around the weight room.

"You can give 'em," Taylor said, "but don't go gettin' 'em back. Understand?"

"No," someone answered.

"Good." Taylor smiled.

He didn't look much older than the kids themselves, even though he was thirty and had fathered two children. Rusty stood well under six feet tall, wore a boyish grin, and had never played high school basketball. He wasn't a good shot on the court, wasn't much of a dribbler or much of a passer, but none of that mattered. He was scrappy, funny, outspoken, and an invaluable presence in the locker room.

Rusty had qualities you can't teach—fire and desire and an intense willingness to get involved with young people. He had no fear of being made fun of and could say the difficult things that sometimes need to be said in team sports. More important, he could do this with humor. The players would talk to him more openly than to the head coach, Raul Mendoza. Every team needed a guy on the bench like Rusty Taylor.

He was the freshman coach of the Falcons basketball team, as well as a history and geography instructor at the high school. When he'd first arrived at the reservation four years earlier, the kids had taunted him and called him "White Boy." He had absorbed their words without reacting and worked hard to earn their respect. He let them get to know him as a person instead of as a member of a different race. The taunts had faded, and now he was simply known as "Taylor."

He was also the coach of the high school chess team and took that responsibility very seriously. He was still upset because his squad had finished only tenth in the state last season.

"They choked," was how he explained their performance to anyone who would listen.

"Now about cussing," he said to the group. "We don't want any cussing at practice or during games. You cuss and you owe us twenty push-ups."

More protests filtered through the room.

Every player, Taylor said, had to maintain at least a C average in school throughout the basketball year "or at least a very good reason for getting a D." If kids missed practice, they were supposed to bring in a note from their mother or father or closest relative. There was to be no "bad behavior" at any time: no spitting or chewing tobacco or dipping snuff and tucking it into their jaws and getting a buzz that way. The varsity players were not to sit with their girlfriends in the stands during junior varsity games.

"Sit with the ugly guy who's your teammate," he said. "And if you have to sit with your girlfriend, don't hold hands."

Loud boos greeted this remark.

"These are the rules, gentlemen," he went on, "and every one of you will obey them. Any questions?"

Another chorus of grunts rose from the floor, but nobody said anything.

"Good," Taylor concluded. "Then we're all set. We've got a plan, and if you want to be a part of it, come on in and join the team. The door's open."

Rusty sat down and the head coach, Raul Mendoza, stood up. Mendoza was my age and came from a Native American and Hispanic heritage. Both ethnic backgrounds were reflected in his black hair and handsome features. He was short, with a soft voice and gentle eyes. He smiled every time he had a conversation with you, looking permanently glad to have escaped a hard background.

Mendoza had grown up in the small Arizona town of Eloy, out on the barren landscape between Phoenix and Tucson, where the heat is inescapable in the summertime. Alcoholism and tragedy pervaded his family life. He had lost both parents when he was a small boy. He was raised by grandparents and was dirt poor, picking cotton and doing other odd jobs while searching for a way out of the dismal future in front of him.

"If I had fifty cents in my pocket back then," he'd told me. "I was really happy."

As a child, Raul found friends and hope playing basketball. The game made him want to finish high school and go on to college, where he earned a degree in physical education. His size and his talent on the court would carry him only so far, but a teaching certificate would keep him connected to the game for decades to come.

Throughout the past twenty years, Mendoza had been a head coach in Arizona high schools, including the past four at Alchesay. He knew all the dangers and pitfalls of his profession. He'd been cursed at by parents because he'd cut their kids from the team or wouldn't play certain boys as much as their mothers or fathers wanted. People had stood outside of locker rooms and tried to intimidate him verbally and physically when he came out because they felt he wasn't treating their sons right. He'd even been threatened with a lawsuit over his coaching choices.

"I learned a long time ago," he often said, with a grin lighting up his face, "to just walk away from them and let it go."

He tried to dismiss the difficulties, but they hurt him more than he let on. It would take a good part of the season to learn just how deep the hurt went.

Mendoza and I shared some common ground. For many years, his coaching hero had been John Wooden, the man I'd played for at UCLA when our team had captured three straight national titles in the late 1960s. Wooden's formula for winning was called the "Pyramid of Success"—a triangular chart that I'd studied and tried to put into practice throughout my career. Coach Mendoza kept a drawing of this pyramid in his office, and he had known some success.

Last season, his team had finished runner-up in the 3-A state tournament, which was held at the America West Center in Phoenix, the home of the NBA's Phoenix Suns. Alchesay had had an excellent player named Armando Cromwell, the best basketball player ever at the school according to many longtime observers of the program. The Falcons had lost the championship game by only three points. They could have won, but they missed two free throws and a couple more shots in the final seconds. It was a bitterly disappointing defeat, one that people in Whiteriver were still grumbling about. Even though Cromwell had graduated and gone on to play small college ball, expectations were very high that the Falcons could win the state this year.

"All right," Coach Mendoza said to the players, "you've got to change certain things if we want to have success. You've got to change some habits. You can't stay up late anymore. You can't sit on the couch and watch TV until 2:00 A.M., eating potato chips and drinking pop. You've got to cut down on all that and get in shape. You've got to make a commitment to the team now. Last year, we lost our point guard because he made some bad choices."

One bad choice had been to drink alcohol; because of this, the point guard had been kicked off the squad. Many people felt that his absence had cost the team the state championship. He was hardly alone in his problem. Alcohol abuse had been as widespread on the basketball roster as on the reservation itself. Only four players on last year's Alchesay team had not been involved in some form of substance abuse. That didn't surprise me. I'd grown up around the same things in Harlem. The guys in the neighborhood or at my high school, including some talented athletes, had consumed large quantities of Thunderbird wine and smoked marijuana. Kids on the reservation may have been more drawn to beer or hard liquor, but the goal was the same: escape from your own life for a little while and feel better—or at least dull the pain.

"Coach Kareem?" Mendoza asked, glancing at me. "Would you like to say something?"

I nodded, then faced the guys for the first time. I had pre-

pared no speech. Throughout more than three decades in basketball, I had never been much on locker room pep talks, and
that wasn't going to change now, but I felt that a few words—
a very few words—were in order. I opened my mouth and the
room became silent.

"I want you to understand," I said, "that I want to be here.
I have chosen to do this with you and we're going to go forward
together from this point. I hope this is a great learning experience for all of us. That's it. Thank you."

"Okay," Mendoza said. "Let's go outside and do some running. Let's see who's in shape."

The meeting was over. Everyone walked toward the door, the
players going out together as a group, with the coaches following behind them. In addition to Mendoza, Rusty Taylor, and
myself were the team's two other assistant coaches: Rick Sanchez and Tommy Parker, who were cousins and basketball fanat-
ics. Rick, the junior varsity coach, taught information technology
at the high school, while Tommy was a house painter in
Whiteriver.

Both had played basketball at Alchesay, and Tommy, although he was only a little over five feet tall and had put on a
few pounds in recent years, had once been a local star. He had
a son, Joe, who was trying out for this year's squad, and a
daughter, Shasheen, who was going to be our student manager,
taking care of the basketball equipment and some other tasks
for the Falcons. Tommy and Rick had been involved with the
team in one form or another most of their lives. They could talk
about the past glories of Alchesay basketball with endless sup-
plies of knowledge and passion. The team's place in the commu-

nity was far more important than any outsider might have guessed.

We went out onto the asphalt parking surrounding the gymnasium, officially known as the Chief Alchesay Activity Center. More than a hundred years ago, Chief Alchesay had made a deal with the U.S. government that designated the White Mountain region as a military reserve. This had kept the land in the hands of the White Mountain tribe. The chief had been awarded the Congressional Medal of Honor for military action for his outstanding service as a scout. The center named after him was remarkable: a $6 million building that was larger and better than many gyms found at junior colleges. It was just one indication of how big basketball was to the people in Whiteriver.

When I got outside, I looked around at the rustic landscape—the wide open blue sky and pine forests and red rock mesas that rose at the edge of Whiteriver. I loved the West and was grateful for all the things that had started me on my journey to this new place.

THE TRIP TO ARIZONA HAD BEGUN EARLY ON A
cloudy and cool October morning. I'd left my home in Beverly
Hills before dawn in a black Ford Expedition and wound my
way through the endless L.A. traffic, heading east. It had taken
many miles to put the cars and smog of Los Angeles behind me,
but by the time I'd reached the California state line, Los Angeles
seemed a world away. The flat, sepia-colored desert was quiet
and looked lifeless through the windshield. A few hours later, I
pulled into Phoenix and soon reached the small community of
Miami, where I stopped for gas. As I stood beside the pump
filling the tank, a stranger approached me and smiled, raising
his hand in greeting. There was nothing unusual about this, but
what happened next reminded me that I was not just starting a
new job but a new life.

"Hey, Kareem!" the man said. "How's your team?"

I had to laugh at his enthusiasm. It was October 29, and the
basketball season was still several days away.

"Are they tall?" he asked.

"I don't know," I told him. "I haven't even seen the guys
yet."

"Good luck, Coach," he said, turning to leave.

I watched him go and let the word sink in: "Coach." It had

a fresh and promising ring. During my long career as a high school player at Power Memorial in New York City, a college center at UCLA, and twenty years as a pro in the NBA, I'd been called many things by many people, but 'Coach' wasn't one of them. Change was definitely in the damp autumn air, and not just when it came to basketball. "Coach Kareem." I liked the way that sounded.

I paid for the gas and got back into the Expedition, moving north on Highway 60, getting closer to my new home. As I drove up through central Arizona, the landscape changed, the desert giving way to thin-necked stands of cactus; deep, rusty-sided ravines; and high, reddish mesas. After passing through the town of Globe, with its huge abandoned mounds of mining debris from copper deposits, I reached the Salt River Canyon. This ancient hole in the ground was encircled by sheer walls and evergreen trees. It marked the southern boundary of the White Mountain Apache Reservation and was a clear sign that I was crossing into new territory.

Carefully, I steered the truck down to the bottom of the canyon floor and up its sides, bending around sharp turns and narrow corners, on the lookout for reckless drivers or falling boulders. Emerging from the canyon, I felt the same rush of excitement I always felt when entering an Old West landscape. Back in L.A., I displayed oil paintings of this terrain on the walls of my living room. Looking at them kept me connected to the beauty and history of the region; the real scenery, though, was always better.

The land appeared much as it did in the last century. Only power lines and paved roads gave evidence of the modern world. Hawks flew overhead, and the woods alongside the road were thick with elk, cougar, wild pigs, and bears. The Mexican gray wolf had lately been reintroduced into this environment. I liked the thought of this great animal hunting and surviving and thriving in these ponderosa pine forests. The gray wolf had nearly been exterminated, just as the Apache and other Native American tribes had in recent times. But they too had found a way to live and were still trying to adapt to contemporary life in the United States.

White crosses with names painted on them stood by the shoulder of the highway, designating where people had been killed in car wrecks. Some of the dead, I would later learn, had been Native Americans who were driving drunk.

I entered the reservation and pulled over, shutting off the engine. Stepping outside, I took in the land, the ancestral home of the White Mountain Apache tribe. They'd come to the Southwest from northern Canada, where they'd been known as the nomadic Athabascans. They'd come here centuries before the American Revolutionary War, long before the English colonists landed at Plymouth Rock, and more than a hundred years before Columbus sailed for what would become America. Since around 1350, they'd been roaming these forests, hunting the local game, and growing crops in these fields.

My vision of the past was broken by the sound of an eighteen-wheel timber truck barreling down the road toward me, carrying stacks of just-cut pine logs. I got back inside the Expedition and drove on.

MY JOURNEY to the White Mountain Apache Reservation hadn't really started that morning in Beverly Hills, but further back in time, well before I was even born. My father's family came from Trinidad in the West Indies and had members who were Carib Indian. My mother's family was from North Carolina, and she was part Cherokee. I was not only African-American, but one-fourth Native American, and my identification with the Indian people had always been mysteriously strong and deep. I always wanted to know more about these aspects of my background.

As a boy I would often wonder about my connections to these tribes, but I couldn't find any accurate information about either the Carib or the Cherokee in the books I read or the Westerns I saw on television. Indians, real Indians leading real lives, had been written out of the American past, especially when it came to the entertainment industry. The ethnic makeup of the cast of one of my favorite TV shows, *Rin Tin Tin,* had nothing to do with how things had really been. There were no Chinese railworkers or Hispanic people depicted, no African-American military personnel ("Buffalo Soldiers," as they were called) in the U.S. Army, and the Native Americans were little more than degrading stereotypes.

Television had completely glossed over the shameful facts about the American government's dealings with the indigenous population of our country—and when it came to TV and movies, the Apache got the worst of it. They were almost always portrayed as bloodthirsty savages. Why some of them had been determined to fight back against the culture that was invading them or why they had tried to preserve their freedom and way of life had been buried.

As I drove toward the reservation in the fall of 1998, all of these things were on my mind. I was about to start coaching basketball, which I'd been hoping to do for some time now, but

I would also be fulfilling other long-held desires. I would be working with minority youngsters, exploring the history of the region, and getting to know more about another culture—a culture that, despite Hollywood's efforts to ignore or demean it, I very much admired. General Colin Powell had recently been speaking publicly about the need for people to perform volunteer work for others, so I'd decided to do my part.

I could hardly believe I was here. In my boyhood in New York City, I'd fantasized about living by myself out West and being able to do the things I wanted to do every day, like living around Indians and riding horses and taking target practice with my firearms. Back then, it had never occurred to me that such dreams could come true, but now that they were, I was as excited as a kid.

After traveling through miles and miles of forest, I entered the town of Show Low, about three miles north of the reservation's edge. I slowed down and drove along the main street, Deuce of Clubs Avenue. Show Low had been born straight out of a Western legend. Back in 1870, Marion Clark, a white settler, and Croydon Cooley, a famous Western scout, were partners and homesteaders in this neck of Arizona, controlling 100,000 acres of land. The story has it that when the two of them got into an ugly squabble over money, they decided 100,000 acres wasn't big enough for both men. They resolved their differences not with fists or revolvers but with a card game called Seven-Up. The winner would buy out the loser's land and the loser would find another place to live.

They played all night and were about dead even; by the last hand, Cooley needed only one point to defeat his opponent.

Clark looked across the table and said to him, "You show low and you win."

Cooley cut the deck and showed the deuce of clubs. "Show low it is," he said, beating his ex-partner out of all the land and naming the future town where the card game was unfolding. Cooley added to his legend by going on to marry three Apache women and became the only white person ever buried on the reservation.

From Show Low it was just a few more miles to what would be my home for the duration of the basketball season: a condo by Rainbow Lake in the village of Lakeside, Arizona. When I reached the edge of this small community, I drove through some gates and pulled into the condo's driveway. Flying by the lake's shore was a big bald eagle, cruising the water for its evening meal. I switched off the engine, and the great bird turned toward me and stared, offering its welcome and reminding me that I was not in L.A. anymore, but right next to the 1.6-million-acre White Mountain Apache Reservation—right where I wanted to be.

I couldn't wait for the first practice.

■\\\\■ FOLLOWING THE SPEECHES IN THE WEIGHT ROOM, I had walked outside with the other coaches to watch the kids run around the activity center. Mendoza asked the prospective players to line up in rows in the parking lot; he wanted to see if any of them could finish a mile in less than six minutes. The boys bent over, put their hands on their knees, and took off around the big reddish building where some of them would be playing basketball this season. It was a spectacular facility for any high school, but especially for here on the reservation, where many people were homeless and many of the homes themselves were ramshackle or slowly deteriorating.

The Chief Alchesay Activity Center had cost $6 million and was designed in the circular style of the traditional Apache dwelling known as the wickiup. The tribe doesn't like square structures and avoids building them whenever possible. A local man had recently told me about a new elementary school for White Mountain Apache kids that is two round buildings placed side by side.

"From the air," he had said, "they look just like Dolly Parton lying on her back."

The tribe wanted the gym to reflect a couple of things: a distinct Apache identity and just how much they valued their high school basketball team. Only the rodeo equals basketball in popularity on the reservation. Nineteen miles north of the center is the Hon Dah Casino, owned and operated by the tribe (*hon dah* means welcome in Apache). As part of a loan package for the casino, the tribe had borrowed an extra million dollars and used it to install a state-of-the-art basketball floor for the activity center.

The gym seats about 5,000 and is of junior-college size and quality. The walls and huge ventilation pipes are painted different shades of blue or beige and the floor has a rich shine. The court is six feet longer than a regulation high school floor, which is legal under Arizona state rules. At first I thought that Alchesay officials had done this in order to make the court the same size as a college or pro court, but there was a more important and subtle reason. Since I hadn't yet seen the team practice, I didn't know what it was.

The first group of boys was coming around the center. None were going very fast, but all seemed to be working hard. I'd been told about some of the players and was still trying to match names with faces. I recognized Kyle Goklish, a senior guard and one of the team leaders. As a freshman, he'd lettered in five sports—basketball, football, baseball, track, and cross country—and had repeated this feat in each of the following years. He was also an excellent student, maintaining an A average. Kyle was not large, but he looked powerful. He wore a calm, focused expression and had been described as a quiet, self-contained young man.

I also recognized Tony Parker, another guard who had been a starter on last year's team. He was about the same size as Kyle, but didn't seem as centered. He was related to both

Tommy Parker and Rick Sanchez, and some people had said that Tony was just the opposite of Kyle: a fiery kid who displayed a lot of emotion on the court and liked to speak his mind—a bit of a rebel. These two talented guards were considered the Falcons' best players and were expected to carry the team back to the state tournament.

A couple more probable starters came running by: Brennen Butterfield and Loren Lupe. Brennen was six feet, two inches tall and thick through the chest and shoulders. He was a serious-looking kid who, I'd been told, had a tendency to get down on himself during a game. Some players need to be criticized in order to play better, but some are so self-critical that pointing out their mistakes has a negative effect on them and makes them withdraw. Brennen, according to Rick Sanchez, fit the latter category. His father and older brothers had played sports before him at Alchesay, and all of them had been called "Butter." Naturally, Brennen was also known throughout Whiteriver by the same name.

Loren Lupe, like many of the kids on the reservation, was known for being almost completely silent, at least around adults. The Apache are not a very verbal culture, and some of the players would take weeks before saying hello to me; they acted as if they needed permission to speak. I'd noticed Loren earlier in the weight room, and he'd appeared inward and shy, protected by all kinds of invisible shields. He reminded me a little bit of myself at that age. People said he was (also like me) a passionate reader who enjoyed being alone with a book, plowing through Shakespeare, Sir Walter Raleigh, and his other favorite author of the moment, John Grisham. Breaking through his si-

lence and trying to communicate with Loren and the other players would be the biggest challenge I would face all season.

These four kids, basically two guards and two forwards—although Butter could play the center position—were supposed to
make up the core of the team, but our fifth starter was still
unknown.

The boys were chugging hard around the gym, and I glanced
down at my stopwatch to see how they were doing. A few were
on pace to come close to six minutes, but most were lagging far
behind. None appeared to be in good enough shape to run the
court for very long, and watching them jog across the asphalt
gave me no indication of how they would play basketball. If you
had asked me at that moment to guess their style of play, I
would have been utterly wrong.

I gazed up from the stopwatch and shaded my eyes from the
brilliant autumn sun. Whiteriver, a spread-out village of 3,000
people in a small valley, was 5,390 feet above sea level. The
light here was intense, clear and sharp enough to sting the eyes.
The air was so clean you could taste its freshness, at least compared to what you breathed in L.A. The air was so thin in this
part of Arizona that since arriving in Lakeside, I'd had trouble
sleeping because my body had not yet become acclimated to the
elevation (and because I was anxious to get the season started).
Being here reminded me of playing against the Denver Nuggets,
whose arena is 5,280 feet above sea level. Whenever the Lakers
had traveled to Denver for a game, I'd ordered a supply of oxygen to be delivered to my hotel room so I could get some rest.

As the boys continued passing by, I studied them as a group.
They were all remarkably similar in size—about five feet, ten

inches tall—and many had the same physique. They were trim and thinly muscled, with little excess weight, looking agile and slight, but strong. They had short dark hair (except for the rat-tails that hadn't yet been shorn), high cheekbones, and serious eyes. Their faces seemed old for their age—much older than the teenagers I saw wandering through the malls in L.A. When they frowned or strained from the exertion of running, they conveyed some of the old pride and fierceness of the nineteenth-century Apache braves.

"The basketball team," Alchesay superintendent John Clark had told me, "are our warriors of the 1990s. When they play basketball, they evoke the kinds of things their ancestors did."

I didn't know exactly what he was talking about, but I was about to find out.

Because of his height and coloring, only one kid stood out from the bunch. Ivan Lamkin, six feet, six inches tall, was white, and last summer he'd transferred into the school from Lecompte, Louisiana, for his senior year. He'd grown up in this part of Arizona before moving down South and then coming back to Whiteriver with his mother, following her recent divorce. At first he worried that the kids on the reservation might not accept him because he looked different, but after joining the football team and befriending a couple of players, his worries gradually went away. His Apache teammates had given him a nickname, which not only signaled that he was welcome, but that they had a sense of humor. They called him "Big Sexy."

Ivan ran in an awkward, lumbering way. He was still growing and might add a few more inches—and maybe a few more pounds—before he was through. He looked unpolished, and people said he was still learning the game, but maybe, just maybe. . . . From the moment I saw him, I held some secret ambitions for Ivan, some dreams. I was hoping that with my coaching help, he might develop and even become an All-State player. I knew this might be unrealistic, but these thoughts were part of my makeup. Because of my own size and experience as an athlete, no matter what level of basketball I'm involved with, I gravitate toward the big guys and want the best for them.

Maybe Ivan could be our fifth starter. We needed a center, and we badly needed some height, because we were going to be shorter than nearly every team we went up against. He might be the missing piece that could edge the team toward its ultimate destination—the America West arena in Phoenix.

Out of the corner of my eye, I noticed Edgar Perry coming toward me across the parking lot. He smiled his wide, handsome smile and shook my hand, welcoming me to my first day on the job. I stopped watching the runners for a while and chatted with him in the warm afternoon sunlight. No matter what I was doing I always had time for Edgar, because without him I would not have been in Whiteriver. It was Edgar who'd really kick-started my coaching journey to the reservation, with some help from Mad Mountain Mike.

— IV —

■ MY FRIEND MIKE GULI LIVES IN THE HILLS OUTSIDE
of Fort Collins, Colorado. He's a high-country mountain man
and, like myself, a native New Yorker with a magnetic attraction
to the Old West. Mike makes a living as a designer of modern
Western-style clothing, which he sells in his store in Fort Collins. For many years he's conducted his own research into Native American culture and has developed many contacts on
various reservations.

I got to know Mike in the mid-nineties, when I was working
on a book called *Black Profiles in Courage,* about several African-
American heroes obscured or forgotten by history. Some of these
individuals, from the Southwest explorer Estevanico to the civil
rights protester Rosa Parks, changed our country for the better
but were almost lost to posterity. One such group were the Buffalo Soldiers, the black troops who had been stationed at Fort
Apache, just five miles away from the Chief Alchesay Activity
Center in Whiteriver. In my travels I've learned that people all
over the world know Fort Apache, but mostly from the movie of
that same name, starring John Wayne. I wanted to know more
about the fort than Hollywood had ever told me, so I began
digging into the rich past shared by African Americans and Native Americans.

By the late nineteenth century, African Americans already had a long and distinguished record of military service to their nation. They had fought with George Washington against the British and for Abraham Lincoln against the South (33,380 black men had died in battle in the War Between the States). In 1866, the year after the Civil War ended, Congress enacted legislation that created the Twenty-fourth and Twenty-fifth Infantries and the Tenth Cavalry. They became known as Buffalo Soldiers, being so named by the Native American groups—Southern Cheyenne, Comanche, and Kiowa—who were gathered at Fort Sill, Oklahoma. They were employed by the U.S. government at thirteen dollars a month. For the next two decades, they fought the brutal Indian and Mexican border wars throughout the Southwest.

The Apache were the last tribe to resist the advancing U.S. Army. The White Mountain Apache never surrendered to the United States, never signed a peace treaty, and never relinquished title of their land to the American government. In 1872, instead of giving up to the opposing military forces, the tribe made a deal with the government that allowed them to keep their land, an area forty-five miles wide and seventy-five miles long in eastern central Arizona. Many of the Apache became scouts for the U.S. Army, working as partners with the federal government rather than against it.

But some Apache rebels—led by Geronimo, Juh, Nana, Victorio, and Mangas—would not accept the conditions of the treaty or the shabby treatment they received from the American military. They kept fighting in the region for fifteen years, far longer than any of the other Native American insurgents. Geronimo himself, the most famous and defiant of all the Apache warriors, wound up performing in a Wild West show. One day, at the age of eighty-five, he fell off his horse drunk and landed in a patch of muddy water, dying from exposure.

In 1888, the renowned frontier painter and sculptor Frederic Remington came to Arizona and rode with the Tenth Cavalry. He wrote of his travels in *Harper's* magazine and did numerous drawings and paintings of the Buffalo Soldiers and Apache scouts. The Wild West Museum in Cody, Wyoming, holds an excellent exhibit of his work and some Tenth Cavalry memorabilia. The legendary filmmaker John Ford also made a tribute to the black cavalrymen called *Sergeant Rutledge,* starring Woody Strode and Rafer Johnson, one of the few movies ever made that tried to capture some of the nineteenth-century interaction of African Americans and Native Americans.

The two groups have had a long, deep, and complicated history together. Some Indians had owned slaves. Some had done battle to free them. Some African Americans had hunted down the renegade Apache in the Southwest, but had carried out this effort in cooperation with the White Mountain Apache scouts. While chasing after Geronimo and other rebels, the Buffalo Soldiers and White Mountain Apache scouts had risked their lives for one another in order to capture men they both perceived as their enemy. Some Buffalo Soldiers had settled down in Arizona and raised families near the Apache reservation, while others had married Indian women, leaving behind a small but permanent African-American influence.

I was fascinated by how the two cultures had intermingled back then and how so many of their stories had been left out of our history books. Mike Guli was interested in many of the same things and encouraged me to pursue these subjects. I told him that I wanted to visit Fort Apache to do research and that I was looking for a very particular piece of information. I asked if he knew anyone in Whiteriver who might show me around.

Without hesitating, he said, "Edgar Perry."

IN 1995 I met Edgar at the Fort Apache Cultural Center. His own grandfather had been an Apache scout for the U.S. Army, which was how he got his name. "Perry" had been the name of a cavalry officer who had befriended Edgar's grandfather and his family. Many of the Apache families back then had been referred to by numbers, because no way had been devised to translate their Apache names into anything approaching English. Many others in the White Mountain tribe had taken on Spanish surnames during the period of Spanish and Mexican occupation of the Apache territory.

Edgar was full of historical information about the tribe and the fort, and I was immediately struck by his appearance. He had the classic look of the Southwestern Native American and resembled many of the Indians I'd seen in the Randolph Scott movies I'd watched when growing up. After viewing those movies, the kids in my neighborhood would go outside and play-act the things we'd just seen. The parks of northern Manhattan would be alive with Billy the Kid wannabes. The mystique of the Old West was alive in those woods. We would pick new heroes with every film, and our group was full of eager buckaroos. I always felt closest to the lawmen in these movies, like Bat Masterson or Wyatt Earp, because my father was a police officer in New York and had a gun. (Because of him, I have always been comfortable around and owned many firearms.)

Edgar was in his sixties and had long silver hair and a deeply creased, weathered face. His cheeks had the symmetrical lines common among the Apache, and his eyes the kind of light that conjured up ancient rituals and wisdom. He always looked as if he were thinking about something humorous. I felt an immediate attachment to the man, and we began to talk like old friends. Edgar was now a tribal leader and had put together an Apache dictionary that was reviving interest in the language among young people on the reservation.

I told him that I was especially interested in a Buffalo Soldier named John Glass. Earlier in 1995, at an antique show in Pomona, California, I'd found an old photo of a black man in Western garb. I remembered his face from another picture I'd seen in books describing black involvement in the settlement of the West. In William Loren Katz's *Black Indians,* he was described as "Jess" and the Indians with him were called "Victorio's Apaches." The same photo had been published in a Time Life book, *African American Voices of Triumph,* and it said that he was a "renegade Negro." The authors speculated that he was a runaway slave who had sought asylum with the White Mountain Apache in Arizona.

The same photo appeared once again in John W. Ravage's *Black Pioneers,* and the text with it said that he was a deserting trooper. The picture that I'd found in Pomona was a solo shot of him—that same individual, and what had grabbed my attention was that he sported a model 1878 Colt double-action revolver, which he wore butt forward on his left hip as opposed to the normal way of butt forward on the right hip. My photo had written on it, "Glass, Chief of Scouts, Ft. Apache, Arizona" and the number "20" scribbled at the bottom. The man's face had captivated me from the moment I'd first seen it. I had to learn more about him.

The problem was that none of the Fort Apache military records were still kept there; they had been sent to the National Archives in Washington, D.C. I decided to take my search there. Glass was becoming something like my Holy Grail, but I couldn't have guessed where my original trip down to Fort Apache was leading me.

After going back to Los Angeles, I stayed in touch with Edgar. Our friendship deepened, and in the spring of 1996, he asked me to visit the reservation for a special occasion. Earlier that year, the Alchesay High School girls' basketball team had won the state tournament, and in May the school was opening its new activity center. Edgar wanted me to come down for the celebration of the girls' victory and to help christen the new gym by saying a few words. I accepted his invitation and drove to Whiteriver. The whole White Mountain community came out to witness the hanging of the championship banner at the gym. I told the crowd that I hoped to return some day to hang another banner from the ceiling, and then I took a ceremonial first shot at the basket. It was a sky hook that fell through the net; the people applauded wildly.

The weekend was turning out to be more special than I had imagined. Edgar wanted me to take a walk with him up to Mount Baldy, about twenty miles east of Whiteriver. This mountain is the sacred peak of the tribe and stands over 11,000 feet above sea level. From the top you can see the orange cloud of pollution rising over Phoenix, 190 miles away. The Apache climb this peak in order to look out over their land in all four directions and offer thanks for what the earth has given them.

We began the trek skyward from a parking lot located part way up the mountain, but it soon became clear to me that I could not keep up with Edgar, who was acclimated to this environment and elevation. Despite his age, he had the footing and stamina of a high-country goat. For twenty years, I'd been in good enough shape to play pro basketball, but Edgar was showing me that all that had ended seven years ago and my life had moved on. As I climbed up the trail, all I could see was the top of his silver head bobbing in the distance. I finally caught up with him at the top.

We looked out in all directions, and then he began to pray. I was very moved by this idea and stood beside him in silence as he gazed up and delivered some words in Apache. Then I turned to the east, toward Mecca, the home of my own faith, Islam, and said some prayers in Arabic.

Unspoken feelings passed between Edgar and me up on Mount Baldy that day, and I had the sense that I wasn't just cementing a friendship with one man, but finding a new set of connections. Although I didn't realize it yet, I was also retracing the footsteps of the Buffalo Soldiers, who had struggled and worked in harmony with the Apache more than a hundred years earlier. I was starting the process of closing an historical circle.

After we descended the mountain, Edgar gave me an eagle feather. (The eagle is the symbol of one of the four clans that make up the White Mountain Apache tribe.) He had asked me to attend the Sunrise ceremony for his grandniece, Shasheen. The Sunrise ritual starts at dawn and marks the passage of a girl from childhood to maturity.

I felt honored by this invitation and went to the ceremony,

spending time with Edgar's immediate relatives and more distant family members from beyond the reservation. Native Americans are now increasingly marrying outside their own groups. There were visitors present from the San Carlos Apache reservation, located south of Whiteriver, and from the Hopi and Sioux tribes, who had come to celebrate the ritual and learn more about White Mountain Apache traditions. Young women from both the White Mountain and San Carlos Apache tribes were being initiated in the Sunrise ceremony.

The atmosphere was very festive. A medicine man and tribal elders gave the young women advice and welcomed them into adulthood. I watched all of this with a good, warm feeling, as if something were stirring inside of me, coming to life. I felt comfortable among these people in ways that I hadn't felt comfortable in many other places. I felt I could just be myself on the reservation and that was enough. At one point, I even stood up and danced with Edgar's relatives, feeling even closer to them now.

That evening the White Mountain Apache men put on masks and crowns before performing their most important ritual—the Crown Dance—in which they imitate one of the animals they respect the most: the deer. The dancers evoked the mountain spirits, leaping and twisting in front of a bonfire as a gesture of reverence for the gifts given to them by Mother Earth. It was a haunting experience, and I will never forget the sights and sounds that I absorbed by the light of those flames. I left the ceremony at 10:00 P.M. with that glow that comes from being among family and friends. I felt accepted here for who I was.

These people, I was discovering, were nothing at all like the image that had been created in movies and shown to the American public when I was a boy.

THE WHITE MOUNTAIN APACHE TRIBE is matrilineal, which means that women have historically made most of the practical decisions and fulfilled most of the day-to-day responsibilities. They still decide which outsiders can be admitted to a clan. When Edgar's mother welcomed me and asked me to sit by the fire with them at the camp, I knew I was like family.

— V —

I WENT BACK TO LOS ANGELES BUT KEPT THINKING about Edgar Perry and my time on the reservation. Edgar and I talked occasionally throughout 1996. Then, in April 1997, I experienced a wrenching life change. I'd flown to New York for an appearance on the *Late Show with David Letterman.* After the taping, I was talking with some other retired athletes—Reggie Jackson, Walter Payton, and Gordie Howe—when I got a call from the West Coast. My mother, Cora, had just been pronounced dead in a hospital in L.A. You think you can prepare yourself for something like this, but you can't. She had been ill for months and I'd known this was coming, but it was still a sudden, shocking loss.

My mother had lived up to the description of a matriarch. She had been the glue of our family and made sure that all of its members had stayed connected and involved with one another. She had always been there for me, and I'd taken her presence for granted, as though she were always going to be there. It was my mother who had dealt with the day-to-day aspects of instilling discipline. My father had simply backed her up. It was my mother who had known how to get me to do my homework and not duck my other responsibilities. She knew just how many demands were enough to make and how many were too much. She was strict but loving. Now she was gone and I felt depressed and confused. The debilitating effects of her illness and death on me were more than I could measure.

A week or so before her passing, I had been driving to a hospital in Century City, where I was going to meet my father and make the decision to take my mother off a life-support system. She was semicomatose and her doctors had said she could not recover. My father had not wanted to be the one to tell the medical staff to unplug the machine and end her existence, so that duty fell to the rest of the family. On my way to the hospital, a man stopped several cars ahead of me in heavy traffic on Olympic Boulevard. He was waiting for a parking spot to open up and delaying everyone who was behind him.

People began honking at him to move and I did too, but he just sat there and did nothing until he was able to park his car. When I finally drove past him, he flipped me off. I was under enough pressure without that. His gesture opened the valve for all that pressure to be released, and for the next few minutes, I simply lost it.

He'd stepped out of his car, and I stepped out of mine and walked up to him. We stood face-to-face exchanging words and getting more and more enraged. I grabbed him and his feet slid out from under him; his toupee fell off, and he landed on the pavement. When he got back up, I was still holding on to him, and we were shouting.

For the first time, I took a good look at him. He was about my age, but much smaller—a total stranger whom I had locked in my grip. I realized that we were two grown men fighting over a minor traffic incident in the middle of Los Angeles.

Why was I here? What was I doing? What had caused me to stop and grab him?

I let him go, but it was too late. He sued me and pressed charges because I had physically restrained him. He wanted to take action that would have given me a record, but that was unacceptable. I hadn't intended any harm. I hadn't planned on hurting anyone. I was just more frustrated than I'd imagined. Things had been building inside of me for months—things having to do with my mother and with living in L.A. and with feeling that it was time for me to make a change, but not knowing what I wanted to do next.

I certainly didn't want to be doing this.

In time, the man and I came to an agreement. I would take a six-week anger-management class overseen by the court system, and he would not file suit against me. I was not prosecuted and eventually paid him a settlement.

Immediately following this confrontation I'd driven on to the hospital and met with my dad. I then made the decision to take my mother off the life-support system, which the doctors did three days later. Ten days after that, she was dead. It was time to regroup and think about the future.

It had been easier for me to confront a stranger in a parking lot, than to deal with the loss of my mother and some other things that had been going on within me.

For years before this, I had wanted to take a break from Los Angeles, and had been making new friends in other places. L.A.'s celebrity world had never had a big hold on me, and what I was really looking for was more of a community feeling. In some ways, I'd found that when I'd lived in Hawaii during pro basketball's off-season. I was ready for a change. My kids were all grown and had moved out of the house. I had no pressing business deals that were keeping me tied to L.A., so my reasons for staying there were few. I sensed that I was preparing myself for something new, but it hadn't yet taken shape.

After my mother's funeral, I was withdrawn for a long time and thought about many things. I understood that I was getting older (following my mother's passing, I was the one who now had to take over part of the difficult task that she'd been doing until recently: caring for my elderly father). I was fifty now, eight years out of professional basketball, and there were things I hadn't done that I still wanted to accomplish. It was time for me to figure out my priorities and get busy moving forward, but for months I remained unfocused and despondent, grieving my loss.

I rented a condo in western Colorado, where I own fifty-five acres, and took along my writing tools and some research materials. I liked being near the mountains and away from L.A., enjoyed keeping a journal, and had a lot of time to think. I kept remembering my mother and looking back at all my parents had done for me. I grasped a very basic thing: All my life, I'd been blessed by having great teachers, starting with my mother. At every step of the way, from early childhood through grade school, high school, college, and on into adulthood, an elder had always been there to show me the way to work on my game and my life.

My first and most important teacher had now died, and the truth was staring me in the face: I was becoming an elder myself. I was more than old enough to be a teacher or a tribal leader, and my tribe, stretching all around the earth, were the people who made up the world of basketball. For nearly a decade, I'd stayed away from the game that had given me more than I could have ever imagined. It had provided me with a career and financial security, with friendships everywhere and a sense of connection and purpose. It had given me an identity around the globe.

I'd walked away from all that because after twenty years in the NBA, I was burned-out. Two decades of constant traveling, living in hotels, and being prodded by coaches and screamed at by fans had taken a serious toll on my body and nerves. I was exhausted and needed time away from the sport and everything associated with it. For a while, I concentrated on other ventures—making movies, writing books, and fund-raising—but slowly my desire to be involved with the game returned. In the mid-nineties, I'd done hoops clinics in Hungary, Indonesia, Russia, China, and Brazil, but that wasn't enough anymore.

Certain aspects of the game were being lost—especially those having to do with how big men should play basketball—and I didn't like that change. The way I'd been taught to approach the sport was fading, and I felt that something valuable was being forgotten. I wanted to get back into the game and into the lives of others.

Over the past few years, I'd put out feelers for coaching positions in the pros or at the college level, but none of these efforts had come to fruition. Pro and college executives seemed to be looking for people who had come up through the ranks as coaches or who had always stayed attached to the game. I didn't fit either of those profiles. I had never coached anywhere, except at some clinics or in specialized sessions with several big men, such as the first pick in the 1998 NBA Draft, Michael Olowokandi, the seven-foot-one-inch center from Pacific. And throughout the 1990s, I had gotten away from the sport in order to move in other directions. I was a loner, people said, who didn't fit the corporate mold that some universities or pro franchises were now pursuing. Getting back in the game was more difficult than I'd thought it would be.

My grieving period had ended and I was more ready than ever for a new challenge.

IN THE SPRING OF 1998, Edgar Perry visited my home in Los Angeles, which is filled with nineteenth-century Western and military artifacts: guns and swords and saddles and uniforms, tomahawks and knives and drums, buckskin outfits and paintings of great open landscapes. Edgar traveled around the country with younger kids from the tribe, dancing at fairs, universities, and other performing venues. Just as I'd danced with the White Mountain Apache two years earlier at the Sunrise ceremony, Edgar now performed another ritual dance at my house in Beverly Hills.

It served as a reminder that I was still attached to him and his people and was always welcome on the reservation. I was still a member of the Eagle Clan. He went back to Arizona, and not long afterward we were talking on the phone.

He asked me what I'd been up to lately and I told him that I was looking for a way to reconnect with basketball.

"What do you really want to do?" he asked me.

"I want to coach," I said.

"Would you consider coaching here?"

"What do you mean?"

"You could coach the Alchesay Falcons—the high school boys' team on the reservation."

I thought he was joking and asked if he were.

"No," he said. "You want me to look into this and get back to you?"

"Sure," I replied, still not thinking he was serious. We set up a meeting where I was interviewed for the position of coach.

The next day I got a call from John Clark, the superintendent of the White Mountain Apache school system, headquartered in Whiteriver. For the past half dozen years, Clark had been a positive force for many changes within the school district.

"You want to coach our boys' team?" he asked me.

"Yes," I said, more certain than I had been previously.

"Do you have a teaching certificate?"

"No."

"If you don't have a teaching certificate in Arizona, it would have to be volunteer work." He paused and laughed. "What's your fee?"

"One dollar," I said. We laughed some more.

"All right," he replied.

"When does practice start?"

"The first of November."

WHEN I'D LEFT LOS ANGELES for the reservation during the last week of October, I had believed that I was going in search of work in the realm of basketball. I'd come to Whiteriver with the intention of seeing if I could successfully coach at this level and if I really wanted to get back into the game. Could I become a teacher and play the role that others had played for me for so many years?

I didn't realize that my time here would have as much to do with teaching the kids about the game of life as about the sport of basketball. I'd come here as much the student as the instructor.

— VI —

THE KIDS HAD FINISHED UP THEIR LAPS AROUND the activity center in less-than-thrilling fashion. The stragglers came in well over seven minutes and everyone was bending over and sucking for high-altitude oxygen. We all went back inside the gym and Coach Mendoza divided the boys into three-somes and gave them some basketballs. He wanted them to run three-on-three drills from one end of the court to the other. Three offensive players would match up against three defensive players. The offensive unit was supposed to pass the ball back and forth as they moved toward the goal for a shot, a standard routine on every team at every level of the game. I'd been watch-ing three-on-three drills my whole life, but what happened next startled me.

Coach Mendoza blew his whistle for the drill to begin and the next thing I knew the boys were flying up and down the floor like pellets fired from a twelve-gauge shotgun. As soon as one threesome had finished bringing the ball upcourt—usually throwing it out of bounds or putting up a wild shot that badly missed the basket—the next three kids got the ball and did ex-actly the same thing. It almost looked like a parody, a fast-forward cartoon version of a three-on-three drill. I looked around the gym to see if anyone else thought something unusual was happening here, but all eyes were on the players on the court, as if this were the way they always did it.

Except for the bouncing of balls and the slapping of tennis shoes on the hardwood floor, the gym was totally silent, the quietest I'd ever heard. Nobody was communicating with anyone else about what was happening on the court. Nobody was trying to slow the drill down and bring some order to it. Nobody was acting as if the players were out of control. Arms and legs were whirling everywhere, players were tripping over one another, and bodies were tumbling onto the floor. It looked totally chaotic.

I watched without saying a word. After forty years of playing and observing basketball, I'd never seen anything quite like this. These kids went from zero to full speed in almost nothing flat. They had only one gear—all out—and stopped for nothing, until they reached the basket or ran into someone and fell down. Then they turned around and ran at breakneck speed the other way. Back in the 1980s, when the Los Angeles Lakers had won five titles in the NBA, we'd been called a running team and we were, but this . . .

This was a new kind of game altogether. It took a few minutes for the notion to sink in: I'd just witnessed my first glimpse of Alchesay Falcons basketball—which was Apache basketball.

IN A WAY, it's more their game than anyone else's. Basketball is not originally a white or a black game, but a Native American one, although most people don't know that. Centuries ago, the Mayans and Olmecs played a form of the sport in Mexico's Yucatán Peninsula. The ball court at Chichén Itzá, typical of most, was shaped like a quadrangle, with temples at its ends and two long walls on the sides. At the northern end of the quadrangle was the Temple of the Bearded Man and at the southern end was the Temple of the Jaguars. High up on each end was a small ring, which was not parallel to the ground, as in today's basketball, but perpendicular. The game they played on this court had religious overtones—and very serious consequences. Scholars believe that the competitors used their shoulders, elbows, hips, or knees to knock a hard rubber ball through the ring, but could not use their hands. Once the ball went through, the game was over and, apparently, so were some other things. The victors won the clothing of the spectators and the losers got their hearts cut out or their heads chopped off. Because the hole in the ring was not large and the ring itself was high up off the ground, a made shot was probably rare and the game was mostly a social ritual. Still, people must have died on those ancient ball courts.

The sport spread throughout Mexico and moved north all the way to Arizona, where the Aztecs traveled and traded with the Native Americans. A centuries-old ball court has been found at the tourist town of Sedona. The "inventor" of modern basketball, Dr. James Naismith, who was living in Springfield, Massachusetts, at the turn of the nineteenth century, adapted the old Indian game to the New World. He nailed a peach basket to the side of a building and cut the bottom out of it. The rim of the basket was placed parallel to the ground and Naismith encouraged players to shoot with their hands. In most places throughout the world, he gets credit for founding a sport that others had been playing in one form or another for hundreds of years before his birth.

*   *   *

AS I KEPT WATCHING the three-on-three drill, I realized that there were obvious reasons why the boys liked to run so much on the court. For one thing, they were going to be shorter than most of the opponents they played who were not Native American. (One of their most bitter rivals, as I would soon find out, was San Carlos, which was to the south of Whiteriver; it had its own Apache squad on the San Carlos Reservation, and in the half-serious parlance of the sports world, these two teams didn't like each other.) Because the Falcons were smaller than other squads, they tried to wear down their opponents with this running style of basketball and win late in the game. They were playing at 5,300 feet above sea level, and if they could sprint like this throughout all four quarters, the other guys would probably collapse.

The Falcons were carrying on a long tradition of running from things that were chasing them or standing in their way. There were legendary stories from the Apache past of their warriors being pursued by enemies and simply riding their horses to death. There were stories of the warriors crossing sixty miles a day on foot over rough terrain and high-country mesas while the U.S. Cavalry aggressively pursued them on horseback, but still weren't able to catch up. There were stories of the Apache covering a hundred miles a day when they had to. A book written about the Apache exploits during the nineteenth-century Indian wars was called *Once They Moved Like the Wind*. Standing in the activity center, watching the boys run up and down the court that first afternoon, I knew that I really hadn't understood that title until now.

The players made a lot of mistakes on the floor. They didn't dribble well, especially with their weak hands (for the right-handed player that's the left hand, and vice versa). Their passes were often amiss. They didn't know how to position themselves under the basket for a rebound or how to use their hips, legs, shoulders, backs, or buttocks to keep other players away from the goal. They didn't shoot layups well with either their weak or strong hands. They tried to grab rebounds with one hand instead of two. (You can reach higher with one hand but have much more control over the ball when you use both.) They weren't physical with one another when playing defense and seemed reluctant to put their hands or arms on their opponents. They shot the ball off the palms of their hands rather than their fingertips. They didn't give the ball the spin needed to keep it on course.

None of this surprised me. Basketball's fundamentals are no longer being taught the way they used to be—at any level of the game. This is why today you see even pro players who can't do some of the basic things mentioned above. I stayed in college for four years and had the fundamentals of the sport driven into me at every practice. Coach Wooden made every player on the team do every single thing involved in the game. He correctly believed that basketball is such a fluid sport that a player could never know when he would be called upon to dribble or shoot or pass or rebound or play defense or do any of a hundred other things, so he always had to be prepared, no matter what happened next.

Those days are past. College stars are not only failing to learn all the fundamentals of the game, as players my age once did, but they are leaving their schools after one or two years to turn professional; the money offered them now is simply too great to refuse. If you can get a $50 million guaranteed contract for having half a game, how can anyone turn that down? What's the incentive to keep expanding your skills? What's the monetary payoff for achieving more success?

Competition in the NBA has suffered throughout the past decade, with virtually no one able even to challenge the supremacy of the Chicago Bulls. Very few impact players, who can carry their team through the playoffs and toward a championship, have entered the league in the nineties. The young guys just aren't getting the seasoning and apprenticeship they need at the university level before climbing up the higher rungs of the sport. Ironically, the country is now full of basketball clinics put on by renowned coaches, clinics that hardly existed when I was starting my career. But these events are mostly just celebrity get-togethers, where you pay your money and can shake a star's hand, but avoid the real task of learning how to play the game.

Big men have suffered the most from all this. The college game is no longer dominated by centers, the way it was for much of basketball's history, and the pro game is now largely a perimeter-shooting contest. Kids love to watch pro stars toss up long-range, three-point jump shots or throw down spectacular, rim-shaking dunks, and that's what they now aspire to imitate. But how many Michael Jordans are there out there? The hard and sometimes dirty work of taking the ball inside and putting up a high-percentage shot near the basket is still the most efficient way of scoring, but it's becoming a lost art.

For a decade, I've watched this trend and been increasingly bothered by it. In the 1990s, only two big men—Shaquille O'Neal and Tim Duncan—have come into pro basketball and made a real impact, but Shaq hasn't developed into a complete player. In addition to that, he hasn't shown much respect for the kind of basketball that was around long before he arrived on the scene. He's publicly referred to the way I used to play as "old man's basketball," which it may have been, but it earned me six more rings than he's got so far.

If the fundamentals were missing from the college or pro game, how could I possibly expect to find them here on the reservation? Trends filter down through the layers of a sport, and the kids out on the floor watched the same ESPN highlights of the three-point shooting superstars that the rest of us did. What did surprise me about this first practice was not just the nonstop running or that the boys hadn't mastered or even seemed aware of many aspects of the game. What struck me was that they played the game virtually without speaking to one another. Nobody talked to anybody about anything.

Earlier in the day, the junior varsity coach, Rich Sanchez, had told me, "At Alchesay, we play ninja basketball. It's silent but deadly. The guys play very quietly and the ball should never touch the floor. Just pass it and run and pass it and run some more. All you should hear is the pitter-patter of tennis shoes as they move down the court together and then the sound of the ball laying off the glass as it goes through the net. Run and play defense and wear the other team down with our quickness and stamina. That's our style."

What I was seeing in front of me was silent all right, but it only looked deadly to their own team.

Communication with your teammates is critical during a game. When I was playing for UCLA Coach John Wooden—who won ten NCAA titles in his last twelve years on the job, a record that most likely will never be challenged—he drilled into us the need to talk to one another throughout the game. If our opponent committed a turnover and one of our players got the ball, he had to let the others know immediately so they could all react at once and switch from playing defense to offense as a group. To signal this switch, we yelled "Ball!" and then everyone knew what to do next. On defense, our players were taught to talk as much as possible, about whom we were guarding and what was happening with the ball. Talking like this was an essential part of the game where I grew up in New York City, and in most other places, and the best teams usually have the best communication skills.

The Apache kids were almost mute on the court. No joking, no ribbing, no verbal horsing around, no telling one another what had just occurred or what to expect next. They shunned talking when they were in motion.

Yet once again, when I took a few moments and thought about it, I realized there were historical reasons behind their actions, things rooted deeply in the story of their own survival for many centuries in a harsh landscape. In order to ambush people or escape from their enemies, in order to stalk food while hunting, their ancestors had mastered the art of silence. That had helped feed them and protect them from their mortal enemies.

Silence had worked well enough in those situations, but this was basketball, and they were hurting themselves (at times, literally) on the floor by not speaking up. Anyone who had ever played street basketball in a big city knew that talking and sometimes "trash talking" to your opponent were as much a part of the action as a good jump shot or a pair of tennis shoes. If your game was good enough, you could get away with saying just about anything.

That custom didn't apply here. I hadn't heard one negative

word all practice—almost no words of any kind. During one of my earlier trips to the reservation, I'd been given a sheet of paper that spells out the dos and don'ts of Apache culture. It's shown to the tribe's youngsters as behavioral guidelines and sometimes passed out to non-Apache visitors who travel to Whiteriver and drop by the White Mountain Apache headquarters. Under the title of "Etiquette of Apache Dos," these things were listed: "Rise early with the sun and pray. Share. Be friendly and courteous. Respect people—the elderly, in-laws, ceremonies, Mother Nature, and the deceased. Tell stories during the winter. Keep home clean. Advise children about life. Learn about clans. Marry outside your clan. Forgive. Stay sober."

Under the title of "Etiquette of Apache Don'ts," it mentioned some things that may have explained the boys' reluctance to talk to one another or bang each other with their bodies on the court. It said not to: "Stare. Point. Whistle at night. Gossip. Be destructive. Misuse words when angry. Waste food. Panic. Make fun of people. Make fun of deer. Push another person. Spit on people. Bump people on purpose. Step over people. Marry into the same clan. Act smart and snobbish. Use makeup [facial]. Chew on fingernails. Get drunk. Lie. Steal. Touch physically unnecessarily. Plan ahead. Make fun of traditions. Pull another person's hair. Be jealous. Kick. Count the stars. Make faces. Be lazy. Bother with things you don't know about, especially Crown Dancers."

And finally it said: "Apache females do NOT participate in sweat hut ceremonies."

I watched the practice, gradually absorbing what I was seeing. It looked like a free-for-all instead of a drill, but I didn't point this out to others or say anything else. It was my first day on the job and I didn't even have a whistle around my neck, because I had forgotten to take care of this detail. I didn't feel in charge without one, but tomorrow that would change, because I would bring a whistle with me.

Also, and more important, Coach Mendoza was still their head man, and he and I were feeling our way toward some sort of shared leadership that would work for everyone. Each of us had not yet defined his turf, although I could already tell that he liked the kind of basketball that was guard-oriented and I liked the kind that included the bigger kids. I was no doubt going to be spending most of my time working with the taller boys like Butter and Ivan.

I looked on that first afternoon and kept quiet, not wanting to heighten any misgivings Mendoza might have had about my being there. Media people were already gathering in Whiteriver to report on the Falcons and my season on the reservation, and I didn't want to make my arrival any more intrusive than it already was.

The practice continued. I felt somewhat amazed, wondering what this experience was going to be like. I wasn't simply viewing a new team playing basketball or starting a new vocation for myself. I was encountering an entirely new culture, a new way of doing things, which was very different from what I had been taught.

There was a great challenge in front of me—much larger than I'd even begun to comprehend.

IN EARLY NOVEMBER, MANY MEDIA PEOPLE CAME to the reservation to report on the fact that I was coaching the Falcons. *Sports Illustrated* showed up, along with *People, Good Morning, America,* and some other print and television outlets. Their wires and camera equipment were strewn across the floor of the gym, and journalists lined the court watching the guys go through their drills. They talked to the players and snapped their pictures and shot footage of them for the evening news programs in Phoenix.

I have never much enjoyed being interviewed, but it was great for the kids to get some attention. It made them feel important to see their faces in national magazines and on TV. My hope was that this exposure might help raise awareness about life on the reservation and the economic and political issues surrounding the White Mountain Apache. It might even help some of their students get accepted into college; the people in charge of admissions at far-off institutions might have heard of Alchesay High because of these media reports, and that might improve the kids' chances of continuing their education.

For weeks after the reporters interviewed them, the kids walked around the school talking about the media and proudly showing off the articles or photos to their friends and family members. The players seemed shocked that journalists working for prestigious organizations would travel halfway across the country to their obscure hometown to write about them or feature them on TV. One scribe hailed all the way from Australia.

The reporters looked shocked at finding themselves on the reservation. They mostly lived in major cities, and Whiteriver is deeply rural. Corn grows in front yards and tethered horses graze right next to houses. Dogs roam freely on the sidewalks, while kids play in the middle of the quiet streets. A little stream—called White River—runs alongside the village. The air is very dry and dusty. The dirt has a reddish tint, like clay. Clothes flap on lines, drying in the piercing sun. The place has a silence that takes a couple of weeks to adjust to.

At the one gas station in the center of the community, which is located by the town's only stoplight, people gather in clumps in the morning, lean on their pickups, and drink coffee from mugs. When I drove by, they smiled and waved, and the kids yelled out, "Kareem! Kareem! Kareem!" I liked the sound of that word bounding around Main Street. I liked it a lot.

Everybody in the village knows everybody else, and no one appears to be in much of a hurry. At noon in the parking lot of the community's one grocery store, Basha's Market, Native American women sit on chairs in the sunshine and peddle T-shirts, backpacks, Pine Sol, crayons, and sweatshirts carrying the logo of the Alchesay Falcons.

The pace here is not just slower, but slowed down. After you've been here for a while, you start to relax in a way that is extremely hard to do in a big city. In L.A. and other places, you acclimate so quickly to the environment that you don't even realize you aren't relaxed. You think that the tension in your body and the buzz in the air all around you is normal, but in Whiteriver the buzz quickly fades. You feel different, quieter both inside and outside. The mind clears, and you start to notice more of your surroundings, the people and the landscape and the stars overhead.

Cattle guards—in the form of metal grates built into the ground—stand at the entrance to the high school. (Cows refuse to walk over these things.) Some personal property in town is enclosed by fences topped with coils of steel teeth. Yards are filled with woodpiles and abandoned junk. Whiteriver has the look and feel of ingrained poverty. In this setting, the $6 million Chief Alchesay Activity Center seems even more spectacular than it is, and the big, white Lutheran church just off Main Street looks like a cathedral. The Lutherans, along with the Baptists and Mormons, have converted a large number of local people to Christianity, but some have hung on to their old beliefs and rituals. Almost all the players on the team came from Christian backgrounds.

The Bureau of Indian Affairs is on one side of Main Street and on the other is the tribal headquarters, a group of low-slung, red-brick buildings. These two sets of offices, working in conjunction with each other, oversee the business of running the reservation. Whiteriver has roughly 3,000 residents and most live in small, brown stucco houses or the frame homes that the government has built here during the past twenty to thirty years. The houses are all shaped alike, in a kind of cramped ranch-style design, with carports and big front windows. They come in a variety of pastel colors: blue, brown, light green, and beige.

"The federal government," says Connor Murphy, who works in town as the director of planning and development services for the tribe, "didn't want to do much of anything around here until the late sixties. Then the Bureau of Indian Affairs got involved as an offshoot of the 'War on Poverty' program and the Indian Civil Rights Act of 1968. They decided to start doing something about the Indian reservations.

"In the seventies, Housing and Urban Development money began to arrive. They started building those little ranch-style, plywood houses you see all over town. They're not very substantial, but they're better than what the tribe had, which was basically nothing."

The federal money was used to build a series of neighborhoods, which the local people then named. They used their imaginations. One is called Bengay, like the pain-relieving cream, because it's mostly inhabited by the elderly. Another is One Step Beyond, because it's near a cemetery. Another is Dark Shadow, because it sits in the shade of some red-cliffed mesas. Others are named Corn on the Cob, Six Pack, and Chinatown, where the homes are very close together.

A thin stream of blue smoke always rises from the southern end of town, on most days the only thing clouding the sky above Whiteriver. It comes from the Fort Apache Timber Company, or FATCO, which began operating in 1963. Before then, many of the White Mountain Apache worked up the road at the McNary Sawmill in McNary, where they learned the logging and lumber business. McNary had come to Arizona from Louisiana. He'd brought black workers with him—the first nonmilitary African Americans in the region—and created a substantial operation in the area. The Native Americans at this plant didn't make much money, but they were getting the necessary experience they needed.

In the early sixties, the Apache decided to start their own mill and harvest the vast forest resources on the reservation. Their 1.6 million acres of land contains part of the largest ponderosa pine forests in the United States.

FATCO, like the Hon Dah Casino north of Whiteriver and the Sunrise ski area to the east, is wholly owned and operated by the tribe. The mill now employs more than four hundred people in manufacturing, logging, and business management, with annual sales of $30 million and a payroll of $7 million. Grandsons of renowned Native American scouts and Indian chiefs now work together in the lumber trade. FATCO ranks in the top sixty lumber companies in the nation and has greatly helped reduce unemployment on the reservation.

Main Street is filled with timber trucks constantly rolling into town, loaded down with huge, just-harvested pine logs and rolling out of town stacked with pallets of two-by-fours or two-by-sixes. If you ask an Alchesay student where his or her mother or father works, or where he or she may one day end up working, you often get a one-word answer: "FATCO."

— VIII —

DURING MY FIRST WEEK ON THE JOB, MANY things about basketball were starting to come back to me as good memories—good sights and smells and sounds. I liked hearing the rubber squeak of sneakers as they stopped and started on the hardwood floor, the murmurs and banter of the guys as they dressed in the locker room for practice: the teasing about girls and the joking that brings young men together as a team, whether it's in high school, college, or the pros. I liked the old smell of sweat that lingered in the air and permeated gyms everywhere, the scent that's left behind after some hard human endeavor has been completed.

I liked standing on the sidelines and watching the players put up jump shots that passed through the net with a perfect swish. I liked being alone in the big half-lit gym before practice started at 3:45 P.M. and jumping rope or stretching my limbs with some yoga exercises or going through old moves on the floor, reliving moments from three decades on the court and hearing the residue of crowds rising out of their seats and yelling. I liked the echo of a bounding ball in an empty gym, bouncing off the ceiling and walls. No matter where I am in the world, basketball courts always feel like home.

*   *   *

BY THE SECOND PRACTICE, I had a whistle around my neck and had begun blowing it. I'd seen enough of the kids' miscues and decided it was time to speak up and start coaching. After watching them run the court wildly and fall all over one another again and again, I stopped the workout and told them several things. Mostly, I told them to think. The difficult part of basketball for young people to understand is that it's a mental game as much as a physical one. I could tell from their movements on the court that they had some talent, but I could also tell that it was largely unshaped and undisciplined.

The players needed to heighten their awareness of one another on the floor, to know where their teammates were at all times and what they were doing. They needed to talk more to one another, so they could cooperate better as a unit. They were no longer five individuals playing alone, but one team. They badly needed to work on the fundamentals of the game, the things that had been driven into me every step of my basketball career: passing, dribbling, playing defense, making layups, taking a good shot instead of a bad one—getting under control.

If they would practice these things during our sessions together, I told the guys, and work on them by themselves, we would have a lot of fun this year and win a lot of games. We could get back to the state tournament in February and maybe even capture the title. As I spoke, the players looked up at me respectfully but asked no questions. They nodded at everything I said and seemed to be listening, but whether they were or not I couldn't be sure. Maybe they were just being polite, the way their customs and Apache forms of etiquette had taught them to be.

After the first two days, about half the kids dropped off the team, knowing they had no chance to make it. Throughout the next week, we cut twenty more guys, to get the number down to the thirteen players who would make up the varsity squad for the 1998–99 Falcons. They were guards Kyle Goklish and his younger brother, Blaine; guards Tony Parker and his cousin, Joe Parker (the cousin and brother, respectively, of our team's student manager, Shasheen Parker); centers Brennen Butterfield, Ivan Lamkin, and a tall kid named Willie Zagotah, who was starting to catch my eye; forwards Loren Lupe and Ernest Burnette, who was known to everyone in Whiteriver as "Tinker"; plus two more forwards, Jon Leonard and Don Ray Johnson, and backups Orlando Aday and Franklin Caddo, a small kid who went by the name of "Punch."

In those first days of the season, while getting to know the players and observing them on the court, I went to Rick Sanchez and sought his opinions about them. He had coached many of them as freshmen and was able to give me a thumbnail sketch of the probable starters.

Nobody knew more about Falcons basketball, or had more enthusiam for the team, than Rick, except perhaps his cousin and our assistant coach, Tommy Parker. At age three, Rick had moved to the reservation when his dad had become Alchesay's principal. Rick had attended grade school and high school here, and then done something very rare in Whiteriver. He'd left the reservation and gotten a college degree in photography at Arizona State University in Tempe before coming back home and teaching the local kids. (Only about 1 percent of those who grow up on the reservation finish college.) In addition to being the current junior varsity basketball coach, he taught information technology at the high school, which included instruction in using cameras and video equipment.

Since early childhood, Rick had played sandlot and then organized basketball in Whiteriver. Like many other people on the reservation, he loved how the game was played in his hometown.

"As a kid," he said, "I remember trying to get into the games and not being able to because our old gym wasn't very big. It only held three or four hundred fans. In the middle of winter on the coldest nights, people would stand outside that gym in a line that was a quarter mile long, just waiting to get in. When I couldn't get a seat, I would stand out in the cold and cry.

"Around here, you just grew up being a Falcons fan. It was the thing to be. If you ask local people who their favorite team is, they always say the Falcons. If you say to them, 'But who's your favorite college or pro team?' they say, 'I don't know. I haven't even thought about that.' Once the season starts, you'll see that we have the best crowd in all of basketball. You'll hear things you haven't heard before.

"We get behind in a game and we make a basket and our fans get up and get loud. We make a steal and another basket, and they get louder. It's unnerving for the other team, and they start to make mistakes. Throw the ball away or miss shots. They're used to seeing a hundred people in the stands at their home games. They come in here and look around and see five thousand very loud fans. They get intimidated, and we've got them right where we want them."

I asked Rick about Kyle Goklish, whom I'd heard so many good things about since arriving at the school.

"He's kind of like our Superman," Rick said. "If someone should get the ball at the end of the game, it's Kyle. Not because his skills are the best, but because his will is so strong. He's all heart and guts. We won't see another kid like him around here for a long time. He's a great kid, a great athlete who's lettered in five sports all four years, and a great student, with a 4.0 grade point in the classroom. He's everything you want in a young man."

I asked about Brennen Butterfield.

"I've watched him and his family members play basketball here for years and years," Rick said. "Another very good kid. Sometimes he gets down on himself too easily. Too self-critical. He has a tendency to go inside of himself and kick himself after he makes a mistake. He'll worry and take himself out of the game by focusing on little things instead of the big ones, but he can play. Good student and serious kid. Whatever you ask him to do, he'll do it."

I asked about Loren Lupe.

"Never says a word," Rick said. "You never know what he's thinking. He's all business, that boy. He's got a good jump shot and uses his body well on the floor. He knows how to block out under the basket and get a rebound. He lifts weights seriously. He knows the game of basketball and doesn't have to talk about it. It's just, 'Here I am and this is what I'm gonna do.' "

Then I asked about Tony Parker, who happened to be Rick's nephew, as well as a relative of Tommy Parker's. Tony was one of those players who struck a kind of attitude on the court, which indicated that he had always done things his way and wanted to keep doing them his way. He had brass, people said, and a lot of it.

"Tony has great instincts for the game," Rick said. "He has an innate sense of when to move. He knows where the ball is gonna be before it's thrown and he's a terrific defensive player. He's got a good outside shot and is very, very competitive. If you're playing tiddlywinks with Tony, he's gonna beat you. He just can't stand to let anyone get the better of him."

From the start, there was a vibe in the air between Tony and me. I could feel it by the second day of practice, when I began asserting myself on the court. I caught him staring at me with some defiance in his face or talking with a teammate when Coach Mendoza or I was trying to make a point. He didn't like to pay much attention to our instructions, as if he really didn't need to hear what we were saying.

He looked proud and young and strong, anxious to test his limits. A part of me admired him for his spirit, but another part knew that if he didn't control this quality—this brassiness—it would eventually hurt him as a player and perhaps long after he'd left Alchesay High. Tony looked like he wanted to prove something, but I wasn't sure what it was. Sometimes I heard him whispering things to the other kids, things which might have been aimed at me. Sometimes, he spoke in a low tone in Apache when I was around, so I couldn't understand what he was saying. Then he burst into a smile.

As the practices rolled along and his behavior didn't change, I wondered if he was making the point that the Apache tribe itself had its own way of doing things and didn't want to be taught by an outsider, regardless of how much experience that outsider had had in the world of basketball—just as his people at an earlier time in their history had not wanted to be controlled or dictated to by a distant government in Washington, D.C. I wanted to take Tony aside and tell him that I was his ally, a friendly force, someone who had come here not to aggravate him but to offer my basketball knowledge. But I also wanted him to know that I had rules and boundaries and I expected people to respect and follow them. One rule was listening when others were speaking; I tried not to interrupt when people were talking and wanted the same courtesy in return. One boundary was realizing that there were consequences for your actions on the floor.

I'd already noticed that when it came to setting boundaries, Coach Mendoza did not send a strong message. If a player made a bad pass, Mendoza let it slide without much criticism. If the same player did the same thing again a few minutes later, Mendoza's response was the same: virtually nothing. This wasn't the way I'd been taught the game. No coach had ever spared my feelings if he believed that criticizing me would make me a better player. The coaches I grew up around all believed that they had to get you out of your comfort zone in order to teach you something. You couldn't stretch your game without feeling the effort, and sometimes the pain, of it. They wanted to keep you off balance, never knowing what to expect.

I thought that Mendoza should have had the kids who were making the mistakes run a few laps around the gym or do some push-ups on the floor, but that wasn't how things were done here. He was lax, or beyond lax, in his discipline. It didn't seem as if he taught the players about consequences at all. In my view, he didn't seem to have their full attention and was letting them get away with far too much.

At the same time, I knew that his position was complicated and different from most other coaches. He was not simply their basketball mentor, but also their guidance counselor at the school. All day long before practice started, he met with the kids and heard their stories about substance abuse—their own or that of other family members; tales of parental discord; self-esteem issues; and teenage problems with academics or the opposite sex. He knew their family secrets. He heard the details about all of their troubles and tried to give them answers as their parent away from home. He was a gentle man and this counselor's role seemed to bring out more of that gentleness. In the process, he became their trusted friend and advisor, their confidant in the adult world, even their protector.

"A lot of the kids," the Alchesay principal, Herve Dardis, had told me, "don't like to leave school in the afternoon. They like to stay here after their final class and just hang out with other kids. This place feels safe to them. It feels good. There's a lot of chaos inside some of their homes, so they try to avoid being there. School is structured, and there's less chaos here."

Mendoza's job was also complicated by something else. He was Native American himself and knew that Apache kids in particular did not like to be separated from the group or singled out for any reason. (The head coach almost always criticized the team as a unit and spoke in generalizations rather than focusing in on specific players.) This tactic was in tune with their culture, and I repeatedly had to remind myself of that once I began to observe the team and its dynamics. Apache prefer to blend in with one another rather than stand out on their own. A number of local people had already told me that because of this quality, the kids are especially prone to performance anxiety when they have to do something in front of an audience.

My role with the Falcons was not the same as Mendoza's. I

wasn't the kids' counselor or their friend (at least not yet). I was still feeling my way toward defining my position on the team. I didn't want to impose myself on the guys—or let things slide too far. I believed in setting boundaries and not letting people cross them, unless they were willing to pay the price. I believed in putting enough expectations on people to make them strive to improve.

Maybe I was old-fashioned, but this is how my mother and father had raised me and how every coach had treated me at every level of basketball, even after I was a seasoned veteran in the NBA. People who think that coaches won't get on you just because you've been an all-star or won some titles haven't been around the pro game. It is not a venture for those with faint hearts or thin skins.

If Tony kept talking at practice and insisting on doing things his way, he and I would probably have conflict. If he changed, then I could do what I wanted to do and concentrate on other things—just basketball things—and put the personality issues aside. I watched him and waited and wondered if he would get my silent message or if that vibe in the air would continue to grow and I would have to spell some things out for him.

— IX —

BY MID-NOVEMBER, MY DAYS HAD SETTLED into a routine. I had hoped to spend more time riding horses, taking target practice, and getting in some cross-country skiing, but the days were already flying by too quickly to do everything I wanted—and it would be a bad winter for snowfall. I was so busy with coaching, preparing for each day's practice in the morning and then driving back and forth to the gym every afternoon and evening, that I barely had enough hours left for other pursuits. Most of my time was devoted to observing the kids.

In addition to the probable starters, some other players were drawing my attention. One was Ernest "Tinker" Burnette. Coach Mendoza had given him a second nickname: He called him "Silk," in the tradition of my old Laker teammate Jamal "Silk" Wilkes, who had been a smooth and productive player. Tinker was a good shooter and played hard, but he had a bad habit of jumping up in the air with the ball before he'd decided what he was going to do with it. Once airborne, he didn't have much time to make that decision. So he often tossed the ball away or threw up a "prayer"—a shot with no hope of going in. Tinker was also known as something of a talker, but he did most of his jawing in the classroom and had a pattern of getting put in detention. Like teenagers everywhere, he really enjoyed goofing off.

At practice, I was constantly watching Ivan "Big Sexy" Lamkin, who I hoped would become our starting center. Ivan had a good, big, strong body and some skills, but he drifted in and out of the action on the floor. One moment you were convinced he could really play, but the next moment he seemed to be sleepwalking across the court, just floating off in his own thoughts. Whenever you offered him some criticism about positioning himself for a rebound or taking the ball up with both hands, he just stared at you or seemed to withdraw further inside himself. I didn't yet know much about Ivan or understand his background and why he was prone to act this way.

Another tall youngster who could play center, Willie Zagotah, was starting to grab more of my time. No one had said much about Willie to me, but my eyes kept returning to him during practice. He was long and lanky, but had some muscle on his frame and some spring in his legs. He was the only player on the team who enjoyed mixing it up under the basket. He wasn't afraid to use his body or put his hands on other players or move them out of the way. (I once asked Loren Lupe to reach out and put his fingers on the waist of the kid he was guarding, in the time-honored defensive move known as "hand-checking." Usually Loren gave no indication of his feelings, but this time his face flushed and doubt came into his eyes; he stopped playing and gazed at me as if I'd told him to go in the locker room and put on lipstick.)

Willie wasn't shy about giving a good bump with his shoulders or hips. The more intense things got in there, the more he was ready for action, unwilling to back down.

He also had a certain style that was appealing. Willie was the last kid on the team to give in to the coaches' orders and get rid of his rattail, and he easily had the coolest haircut on the squad. His hair was pure black, slick and sleek. It was mop-like on top and shaved on the sides. It resembled those old country "bowl cuts," which thirty years earlier had been the definition of square but had now become very hip. When you praised him, Willie never said much. He just nodded or shrugged, but also conveyed the impression that he was aware of more things than you guessed he was and that he wanted to get in the game.

Last year, Willie had had behavioral troubles during the season and hadn't been much of a contributor to the team, but something had happened since then that made him more grounded and serious. In the off-season, he'd fathered a child and was now a young parent. Willie was growing up very fast, and his indifferent attitude had changed. He was ready to grow and learn, and he was discovering his own ambitions. He told people in Whiteriver that after high school, he wanted to become a chef.

Don Ray Johnson was also a kid who made you look his way, but for other reasons. He often came to practice with bruises or cuts on his face and knuckles. He was a fighter, a brawler from what I heard. He liked to get in scrapes over the weekend and show up at practice on Monday afternoon with a new set of scars to display to his teammates. Sometimes, his cheeks were really marked and he looked as if he'd gotten the worst of it. At first, all this was off-putting, but the more I watched him, the more I realized that he wasn't a bad kid and he had some potential on the court. He was a better listener than some other, more talented players on the team, and he reminded me of myself at that age.

When I was in high school, I improved at basketball because I knew I was ignorant about the game. I wasn't afraid to ask questions about anything I didn't know. That was one of my greatest assets. I believed that my coaches could help me, that they wanted to help me, and I understood the difference between ripping someone for no reason and constructive criticism. Don Ray was more open to coaching than almost anyone else on the squad.

He liked to drive the ball into the lane and take it to the basket, but he lacked confidence in his ability to do this. He simply hadn't been shown the right way to make this move, so his skills were raw. He also liked to play inside and mix it up but hadn't been encouraged to develop this part of his game. Don Ray wasn't as physical as Willie but would trade knocks when he had to, and the other guys on the team always gave him a wide berth. To me, he looked like a Native American version of a young and tough Telly Savalas.

BLAINE GOKLISH mostly imitated the things his older brother did. He seemed more interested in studying Kyle's moves than in anything the coaching staff might have wanted to teach him. Jon Leonard, whom Mendoza had initially thought might be a starter, kept getting small injuries that prevented him from practicing or playing in the games. These hurts would continue throughout the season and tie him to the bench.

Joe Parker was a good shooter and would gradually emerge throughout the season as a contributor, especially on offense. His dad, our assistant coach, Tommy, was giving him private instruction and showing him some moves from his old playing days when he was a star at Alchesay High. Joe had an edge that many of the other kids didn't.

Before and after practice, Joe and his cousin Tony enjoyed joking around with Shasheen as she carried out her duties as team manager. They liked to jostle with her and trade verbal gibes. They liked to make fun of her. It was normal, natural, hormonal teenage stuff, but I monitored it to see that it didn't get out of hand. Shasheen was the only female connected to the team; she worked hard and needed someone in her corner.

The last two players filling out the roster were Orlando Aday and Franklin Caddo. Franklin would soon drop down to the junior varsity level, where he could work with Rick Sanchez and get a lot more time on the court. Orlando was an excellent student and had some talent for the game, but the thing I will always remember about him was the strength and power of his face. He was a teenager whose serious eyes indicated that he might have been going on forty-five.

More than any of the other players, Orlando looked like an Apache warrior from the tribe's past, with high cheekbones and a kind of ingrained toughness in his expression. He wasn't nearly as fierce as he appeared to be; he was a bright, friendly kid who loved horsing around in the locker room and laughing with his teammates. Sometimes I would glance his way and imagine him sitting astride a paint pony two hundred years earlier, ready to ride off into the mountains and hunt.

THE PATTERN OF OUR PRACTICES was set that first week of November and didn't change much. The boys were polite when we told them the things we wanted them to work on. They never talked back to the coaches, and they put some effort into doing what we were trying to teach them. But the moment they started to scrimmage, they forgot everything we'd been practicing and reverted back to what they knew best: wild, run-and-gun Apache basketball. They made bad passes, put up misguided shots, missed their layups, and generally played a messy game. I was becoming exasperated but attempted not to show it. Coach Mendoza continued to let these mistakes go in practice, and I continued to wonder what my response should be to his relaxed attitude.

There was a conflict going on, and it wasn't as much within the team as it was inside myself. Sooner or later, I would have to speak my mind, but when was the right time? What if the Falcons opened the season and had great success playing the way they did, just as they'd had last year? Wouldn't it then seem foolish to criticize their way of doing things? Maybe I should let them lose a few games before venting my thoughts. Or maybe I should do it now, before they had the chance to start losing. . . .

All this was new to me, and I was still searching for the answers. In many ways, my past was not much of a road map for what I was encountering. None of my coaches had ever been my friends, at least not while I was playing for them. Part of the reason I'd always wanted to improve my game was simply to shut them up and get them off my back. They had never let me get comfortable around them, and at the time that had bothered me—yet my discomfort had pushed me to improve. I was grateful that they had not let me coast.

Knowing how to make players somewhat uncomfortable, but doing so without harassing them, is part of the balancing act of being a good coach. Red Auerbach, who built the great Boston

Celtics dynasty back in the 1950s and 1960s, came from the old school of motivation. If he felt that someone wasn't putting out in practice or the games, he would walk by his locker and let it slip that another team in a distant city—a city with a team much worse than the Celtics—was looking for a player at this guy's position. The player didn't need this translated. It meant: Start working harder or we'll trade you to a lousy team.

Those kinds of hardball threats are mostly a thing of the past now in pro sports (some players have no-trade clauses in their contracts, anyway). Modern coaches have stopped being dictators and tried to become psychologists. They like to use other motivational or manipulative techniques on their teams. Some people think this is effective, but I always thought of the methods as unnecessary mind games, and I would never want to impose them on anyone I was coaching.

Mind games were one reason I'd needed to get away from basketball for a number of years following my retirement from the game. I was tired of having coaches push my emotional buttons—over and over again—because the season was long and they couldn't think of any other way to motivate the team. To inspire you, they felt they had to anger you and force you to have an enemy. If you were angry at your opponent, the coaches believed, or angry at the referees or at the other team's fans or the media, you would play better. If you were angry at your own teammates or at the coaching staff itself, this was somehow supposed to make you perform at a higher level. So they tried to make you angry and keep you angry throughout the basketball year, which can be about eight months long.

I never bought this concept; I found it annoying and exhausting. There's enough pressure and difficulty in playing a sport in public, where the crowd instantly gives your their disapproval each time you make a mistake, without looking for an artificial way to get you even more pumped up and enraged. I never played better when I was angry, but always did my best when I felt in control of myself emotionally and physically. I never appreciated it when coaches used tricks on me, and I didn't want to do that to the Falcons. If players can't motivate themselves to play the game, then you probably need different people on your team.

ONE DAY AT PRACTICE I decided to run some wind sprints with the kids as a lark. They seemed happy that I wanted to participate in this, and I wondered if I could keep up with them. I knew I wasn't in playing shape, but I jumped rope every day (with a rope that weighed five pounds) and thought I would be all right. I'd forgotten all about the altitude in Whiteriver, and I got a harsh lesson about my need for oxygen-rich air.

We lined up in rows and took off across the court. I ran as fast as I could for as long as I could, but suddenly stopped in the middle of the floor. I was having a near-death experience. I couldn't breathe at all. My lungs were going through the motions but weren't drawing any air. This was scary for me, but the kids thought it was funny and got a big laugh at my expense. Maybe this was good, because they could see that I was a lot more like them than they'd realized. I may have been taller than other people and much older than they were, but I was just another vulnerable human being.

I went back to jumping rope before practice each day and did some jogging near my condo every morning. I wouldn't get caught sucking for air like that again.

— X —

■\\\\\■ I WOULD LEAVE THE GYM AFTER PRACTICE EVERY
day around six o'clock and drive back the thirty miles through
the darkness to my home in Lakeside. I had a lot to think about
and much of it concerned basketball. For one thing, trouble had
been building for years within the pro game and now finally, in
the autumn of 1998, it had reached a bad impasse. The players
had not been allowed to report to training camp because the
owners had gotten themselves into a terrible financial bind by
paying too much money to younger guys who had never proven
themselves in the league. A guaranteed, long-term, $100-million
contract to a rookie who should have been a junior or senior in
college was a surefire way to keep him from ever working on
his fundamentals or really improving his game. The basketball
owners, as in other pro sports in recent decades, needed to be
protected from themselves. Money problems had caused the ex-
hibition season to be canceled and was threatening to wipe out
the regular season as well.

My sympathy was mostly with the players, but I knew that
change was in order for the NBA to thrive. I was a profound
believer in education and in the things that surrounded the educational experience. Athletes need to stay in school until they
have graduated from college. Also, a system is needed in pro

basketball to provide financial incentives to younger players based on their ability to move up the performance ladder and help their teams win. Otherwise, most of them won't be motivated to push themselves on the court. As the lockout dragged on without a resolution in sight, I grew tired of hearing about the money issues in the media. Sometimes a bloodletting is the only way to generate new ideas.

It was especially rewarding for me to be working with the kids on the reservation just now, as the pro game was fighting about billions of dollars and going through a nasty labor war. Regardless of the frustrations I was experiencing with the Falcons, I was glad to be far away from that world of money negotiations and equally glad to be engaged with teenagers and amateur basketball. Worrying about hormonal surges or laying down the law about getting or giving hickeys seemed fun by comparison. The longer I coached at Alchesay, the more the notion of finding a job in pro basketball faded from my mind.

ON THESE EVENING DRIVES back to the condo, a huge orange fall moon rose over the hills to the east of Whiteriver. It sat atop the mesas and shone through the stands of pine that stretched north of town. It illuminated the landscape and made it come alive for me in the darkness, with shadows and ghosts and images of men riding on horseback and old stories of the past. Rolling north along the two-lane blacktop, I turned on the radio and brought in the only station that was clear in this part of Arizona: 88.1 FM, KNNB, which was based in Whiteriver. Local people called it "Apache radio," and it was unlike any other station I'd ever tuned in.

I found it by accident, because my dial was already set on

88.1 FM, the number for the jazz station KLON in Los Angeles. (I'd brought my sound system and parts of my jazz collection with me to Lakeside so I could stay cooked even though I was away from L.A.) On the reservation KNNB was the lifeblood of the community. You could tune in and hear women sharing advice about having babies and raising children and immunizing them against diseases. You could hear about support groups for tribal members enslaved by alcoholism or hypertension. You could hear about how to confront intimate family problems or mental health issues. And you could hear an amazing variety of music, from the country-and-western of Waylon Jennings to the rock of Bob Seger and the reggae of Bob Marley to religious songs about the value of loving Jesus. Christian songs were very popular here, and in addition to the big Lutheran church, there was also a Baptist church in Whiteriver.

The more I listened to Apache radio, the more variety I heard. I was never quite prepared for the next thing that was broadcast over KNNB.

In the evenings, the man behind the microphone regularly switched back and forth between speaking English and Apache without any pauses in between. While talking in heavily accented English, he would suddenly break into the very different Apache language, which seemed to come from the back of his throat and rush forward over his tongue with a rustling noise. It was an eerie, haunting sound that seemed to emerge out of the past, particularly at night as the moon was ascending beside me and the stars were coming out above the reservation and making their timeless patterns in the sky—the same patterns that Native Americans had looked at centuries ago when they were migrating down from Canada or settling in this corner of the Southwest or being chased across a dark landscape by the United States Cavalry.

The disembodied voice on the radio perfectly reflected the mixture of two cultures that history had thrown together in this part of the West. The white and Native American cultures had two radically different pasts, and those pasts had clashed and shaped the Apache experience over the last two centuries. Now they were trying to piece them together into one whole. The White Mountain Apache, like so many other Indian tribes in the modern United States, were living between worlds, with one foot in contemporary America and the other still locked in to their own deep past. They were caught between epochs of time and literally trying to speak two languages at once.

The more I tuned in KNNB and heard the man combining English and Apache, the more I felt that his voice was giving me a glimmer of understanding about my interaction with the Falcons—and their reluctance to change the way they played ball. Much had been lost from their culture and much had been taken away from it. They'd kept their land but given up their old way of life. Basketball had become a part of their new identity, and they had not only known success but had discovered that success by playing their own style. Maybe they didn't want anybody tampering with that style, even if he could help them grow. Or maybe it was still too soon for them to accept the teaching that was being offered.

AS THE PRACTICES CONTINUED and the players didn't seem to be learning much, resisting even the idea of learning, my disappointment deepened. I kept hearing stories about Armando Cromwell, the star on last year's team, who had been the best basketball player ever at Alchesay. His ghost was only making my job more difficult. Cromwell had received great praise for his one-on-one skills on the court and had been celebrated in Whiteriver as a hero. This made it even more difficult to convince this year's kids that team basketball, instead of one-on-one, was the way to go. Every player on the Falcons now secretly wanted to be seen as another Cromwell, the natural athlete who doesn't need much instruction from the coaches—the star who lets his abilities take over and wins the game by himself. But these kids badly needed coaching, and I was determined to give it to them.

Almost every afternoon, I took the big guys—Butter, Ivan, and Willie—down to one end of the court and showed them the George Mikan drill, which I had practiced for countless hours in my efforts to improve my own game.

The kids, of course, had never heard of George Mikan. Most likely, they had heard of very few players from my own era, which had ended in 1989. Back in the late 1940s, Mikan had come into the new pro league known as the National Basketball Association, which had debuted in 1946, and done something that up until then coaches and critics believed could not be done. He'd shown everyone that a truly big man—he was pushing seven feet—could develop the agility and skills needed to play basketball. Before Mikan, players of his size were considered too slow and awkward to be of much value on the court.

Mikan quickly opened their minds. As the center for the Minneapolis Lakers, he led his team to consecutive NBA titles and created the first Laker dynasty (my team had the second one in the 1980s). Along the way, George developed his own drill, in which he would stand close to the goal and shoot the ball off the backboard with his left hand, then with his right hand, then switching between his left hand and right hand again, back and forth, over and over again, until he was scoring with either hand in one fluid motion.

He made himself ambidextrous and prepared himself for using both hands no matter how the ball bounced off the backboard or the rim. He was not only taller than anyone else playing the game, but because of this drill he soon became more graceful and better than anyone when it came to scoring close to the hoop.

His drill is still the best way to learn how to score under the basket. Since Mikan's day, his routine has been passed along to all the significant centers who have played pro basketball. That list includes Bill Russell and Wilt Chamberlain, Willis Reed and Dave Cowens and Nate Thurmond, Bill Walton and Wes Unseld and Moses Malone, myself and Hakeem Olajuwon. You can't score effectively inside in the NBA without using both hands, although many of today's younger players are trying to do just that. This is one reason that the current game has lost some of its dimensions and why the scoring has fallen off so badly in recent years. Take away the productivity of the game's centers, and you take away one of the greatest aspects of basketball.

I showed the Mikan drill to the Falcons' trio of big kids and told them that if they would come to the gym alone and practice it, the technique would make them much better inside players. I also told them that we really needed their scoring if we were going to be a good team. We already had a good outside game, with Tony and Kyle shooting the ball, but if we wanted to compete against bigger teams, Butter, Ivan, and Willie had to produce down low. They listened and would try to do the drill for as long as I was watching them, but I never saw them practice it by themselves, so they never really got much better at it. They just didn't want to be involved with the tedious process of doing something time and again, until they had built certain reflexes into their bodies so they would know how to do these things in a game without having to think about it.

I never expected the kids to pay attention to me because of my career: I'd scored over 44,000 points in the NBA, appeared in eighteen all-star games, and won six championships and six Most Valuable Player Awards. Some of those things had happened when they were around five years old—or, in other cases, before they had been born. To them, I was a figure who showed up on old basketball footage on ESPN2 or *Classic Sports* or perhaps in movie reruns on television.

I was the tall guy shooting the hook shot in some ancient pro matchups, the fellow who back then sported quite a bit of hair. They'd never seen me play live basketball, so I didn't rely on my past as a player to impress them. I expected them to listen to me for another reason. I had learned the game from a series of excellent teachers, starting with my grade school coach, Farrell Hopkins, then my high school coach, Jack Donahue, and then John Wooden at UCLA. I'd learned by studying with the best and was hungry for any scrap of information that could help me. It was these coaches' body of knowledge that I wanted to pass down as part of basketball's great tradition.

I was starting to wonder if this was possible here on the reservation—or anywhere else in the late 1990s. I wondered if the real goal now for many teams was to look good on the court—with their high-top shoes, low-cut socks, and long basketball

pants, the current rage at Alchesay High, as they were every-
where else these days—rather than playing up to your potential.
I wondered if the hunger that had motivated Bill Russell, Oscar
Robertson, and Jerry West, the hunger that had driven Magic
Johnson, Larry Bird, Michael Jordan, and myself, was still there
at any level of the sport.

Everything was bound up together it seemed: both the strike
in the NBA over paying youngsters too much money too fast
and the resistance of many players at every level of the game
to keep learning the fundamentals of their sport. I wondered if
the new world of basketball had passed me by.

One day I went to Coach Mendoza, who is my age, and asked
him about all this.

"The kids on our team," he said, "haven't yet learned the
consequences of their actions. Someday, I hope they do. They
haven't yet learned that what we do in practice affects the outcome of the games. We have talent here, but we're trying to get
them to play smarter and understand the game better, the mental part of it, the commitment and the discipline. They just want
to run and hurry everything. They look at things very differently
from the way I did when I was in school. It's a whole new era
and you have to come to terms with that before you can really
reach them.

"I grew up as a migrant worker in the cotton fields of Arizona.
In high school, I worked long hours on a tractor, and in college
I worked at a copper smelter to pay for my schooling. I didn't
have a lot of talent for basketball, but I studied the game and
learned everything about it that I could. Playing for me was just
like living: a matter of survival. It wasn't just recreation, but
something more. I had to do things on the court to survive as a

member of the team and I was always looking for an advantage. These kids have more talent than I ever did, but they don't feel they have to work that hard. They watch the highlights on ESPN and see someone making a spectacular shot and that's all they want to practice. They don't realize that the guy who made that shot made it just because he's great.

"In my day, nothing was handed to you. As a boy, I lived with my grandmother and got up at 4:00 A.M. I went to work at that hour because I had no choice. When my grandmother asked me to do something, I did it without asking questions. I took care of my half-brothers and sisters and there were thirteen of them. Everything was different.

"When our team goes on road trips now, sometimes these kids have a hundred dollars in their pocket. Somebody's giving it to them for spending money. I can't believe that. I don't know where the money comes from and I don't ask. These are very good kids, but they need to realize that in order to be successful, there's a price to be paid. They haven't grasped that yet."

SOMETIMES DURING THOSE FIRST FEW WEEKS on the reservation, I had to stop and remind myself that the kids on the team were dealing with a lot of other things besides their moves on a basketball court. They were dealing with high school and with being teenagers, but they were also dealing with the recent history of the White Mountain Apache, which had been painful and had filtered down from their ancestors into their own lives. The students at Alchesay High were dealing with some things that other teenagers weren't.

From 1871 to 1922, things had been relatively decent for the tribe. It had stayed attached to Fort Apache and many of the White Mountain men had worked there as scouts, so they'd had jobs and held on to some of their long-standing identity as warriors. No white homesteading was allowed on their land, so they'd also kept control over it. But they were now a colony inside of the United States, and the American government's paternalistic attitude toward them was summed up in a letter written by Vincent Colyer, a commissioner of the Department of the Interior, dated September 5, 1871:

As the White Mountain region has been set apart by the War Department as an Indian reservation, and there are several

bands of peaceably disposed Apache, who have for many years
lived in this country, who can not be removed without much
suffering to themselves, risk of war, and expense to the Government, I have concluded to select the White Mountain
Reservation . . . as one of the Indian reservations upon which
the Apache Indians of Arizona may be collected, fed, clothed,
and otherwise provided for and protected. . . . I would suggest
that 1 pound of beef and 1 pound of corn per capita be issued
with salt daily, and sugar and coffee occasionally.

When Fort Apache was decommissioned and closed nearly
fifty years later, the reservation basically became a welfare state.
The men lost their work and much more than that. They became
dependents of the United States, living on government cheese,
lard, excess cattle shipped in from dairy farms, and sometimes
rancid flour. They ate food that was not good for them and many
tribal members stopped exercising, which they had been doing
strenuously from time immemorial. They gained weight and
contracted diseases, diabetes in particular. When they spoke
Apache in front of white people at school, their feet were shack-
led with balls and chains or their mouths were washed out with
bitter soap. They were punished for doing what they'd always
done and were subjected to forced assimilation into the mainstream culture, even though they had been given almost none
of the tools needed to fit in to that culture.

They felt isolated on the reservation, but leaving their land
and entering the "other" world was often worse than staying
put. They received twenty dollars a month as a subsidy. The
Bureau of Indian Affairs gave them some rudimentary education, but if they learned any skills at all, it was usually how to

clean the homes of whites. The cycle of joblessness, poverty, and despair, so common in urban American ghettoes, had begun here on the reservation. Many in the White Mountain tribe eventually gave up speaking Apache and that further stripped them of their past, their identity, and their sense of themselves as a sovereign people. (The power of taking pride in one's ethnic background cannot be overestimated for minorities. After the Academy Award–winning movie *Dances with Wolves* was released, millions of people came forward and said they had some Indian blood in their veins, because for the first time ever they'd watched their own group's historical experience unfolding up on the big screen, and it had been depicted as positive.)

Since around 1350, when the Apache had moved down from Northern Canada, settled in Arizona, and made the Southwest their home, they had lived in freedom. Now, six hundred years later, they were residents of a welfare state run by a distant, neglectful government concerned with many other things besides the fate of the nation's indigenous peoples. Not much changed until the middle of this century. Then in 1958, the Arizona state government decided that it had an obligation to start educating the kids on the reservations. It began building schools, sending Native American children to classes, and teaching them in English. The Whiteriver United School District Number 20 was created with an elementary division, a middle school, and a high school. (Alchesay High now has 727 students.) The district was headquartered in Whiteriver, with other branches on the reservation.

Apache kids started learning about the American education system and American sports, and gravitated toward basketball. They played the game in school and outside of it. Goals appeared in driveways all over town—old, rickety goals made out of discarded bicycle tire rims that were nailed or screwed into fat pine poles. In the summertime, boys and girls played the game in the heat. In winter, they played on packed snow. They learned the game from their older siblings, who handed it down from one generation to the next, and they entered high school playing it the way everyone they knew had played it. Making the varsity team was one of the fastest ways to earn recognition and respect in Whiteriver, because the town loved its Falcons.

Basketball was something to celebrate and feel good about in otherwise tough circumstances. The reality of life on the reservation lay in the numbers. About 14,000 people, 12,000 of whom were White Mountain Apache, inhabited the area, which includes Apache and Navajo counties. In 1993 (the last time figures were collected), these two counties were, respectively, the sixth and seventh poorest in the United States. Of all households, 52 percent lived below the federal poverty line. Their unemployment rate was 61 percent. Per capita income was $3,805 annually. More than 50 percent of tribal members lacked a high school diploma and only 1.3 percent had a college degree.

Disease was prevalent. One third of the children were obese, which meant that they were much more prone to diabetes as adults. They were also more prone to high blood pressure, kidney disease, and heart disease. Diabetes was so pervasive on the reservation that throughout the mid-nineties, Johns Hopkins University had been conducting an obesity prevention project on the White Mountain Apache and San Carlos Apache reservations.

The National Institutes of Health was funding this research

in order to learn more about the eating habits and activity patterns of Native American kids. They wanted to know which foods the students ate at the school cafeteria and which they rejected. They wanted to reduce the amount of fat in their diets—by decreasing the intake of junk food, like potato chips and soda pop—and increase the consumption of vegetables. Researchers wanted to know how much exercise the kids got on a daily basis and how much time they spent watching TV or movies and playing video games. They wanted to come up with programs that would inform both the students and their families about the dangers of eating bad foods and not getting off the couch.

Researchers hoped to introduce into the school system some traditional Native American games, like hoop toss or relay races or Apache golf, in which you attempt to throw a ball into a ring. They were looking for anything to make the kids more physically active, as well as attempting to preserve parts of the tribe's past.

Obesity was just one problem on the reservation. Fifty percent of the White Mountain Apache people were homeless. Estimates of alcoholism ranged from 40 to 60 percent of the local population. Substance abuse, both drugs and liquor, drove an already high crime rate higher. Homicides averaged one per week, and 32 percent of all deaths on the reservation were alcohol-related. Drunk drivers were a constant threat on the tribe's roads.

"Everyone in Whiteriver," said School District Number 20 superintendent John Clark, "has lost someone to drinking."

Divorce was rampant. Of kids between the ages of ten and seventeen, 40 percent did not live with both parents and 10 percent did not live with either parent. Early in the 1990s, in one year alone, twenty-five tribal members committed suicide.

While homelessness was pervasive, virtually none of the White Mountain Apache was actually without a place to live, because extended families took in those relatives who did not have a dwelling of their own. (When locals spoke about their families, they were not referring only to their parents or their brothers and sisters, or sons and daughters; they were also including their aunts and uncles, cousins, neices, nephews, grandnieces, grandnephews, grandparents, and other more distant blood connections.)

The numbers described a harsh reality. In such an environment, people looked for something to rally around and celebrate. In Whiteriver, they found it in their basketball teams, both the boys' and girls' squads. In 1993, the boys won the state championship. The triumphant players were suddenly surrounded by the kind of adulation and temptation that successful athletes everywhere encounter. Within a year, all the starters had a child on the way.

While there were many problems on the reservation, the biggest was not necessarily poverty, obesity, homelessness, crime, divorce, unplanned pregnancies, or even unemployment. It was education.

"A major concern for us," said John Brach, a counselor at Alchesay High, "is preparing students for college and getting them to stay in college once they're there. We can often find the money to send them to school, but that isn't the largest challenge. Every year we have kids who go away to college but soon quit and come back to the reservation. They've grown up in Whiteriver and have never been anywhere else. Now they're someplace new and foreign, and it's three or four hundred miles away from home. They feel lost and afraid and they want to be around something more comfortable.

"A college environment is very different from Whiteriver, and so are the people. Everything is different and no one understands the kids' background. This is very intimidating for them. The key to their success in school is being able to get an education without losing their Native American identity or their sense of family. The reservation is a family and it has a hold on them that is much deeper and stronger than outsiders realize."

Without higher education, many of the kids can't find work, even when employment is available.

"I can't use local kids for many of the better jobs on the reservation because they don't have college degrees," said Connor Murphy, the tribe's director of planning and development services, which is headquartered in Whiteriver. "We need educated people to run our programs and we want to hire Native Americans, but the great majority of those on the reservation haven't graduated from college. So it's very hard to recruit people from here.

"Kids tell us they don't get encouraged at home to attend college. They don't see people reading or trying to improve their minds. They say they have to fight the system because no one really wants them to go on with their education, even when financial aid is there for them. The opportunities have opened up for them now, but they still have to take advantage of them. Any kid who goes off to college and sticks with it and earns a degree will have a good job waiting for him when he comes back home."

ONE DAY AT PRACTICE, the freshman basketball and chess coach, Rusty Taylor, asked me if I were familiar with the local phenomenon known as a "rescar."

"What's a rescar?" I said.

"A reservation car," he told me. "It's a brand-new car on the reservation that quickly gets a lot of dents in it. Someone buys a new car, and it looks out of place here, so the owner lets it get dirty and puts some dents in it. Then it fits in and is just like everyone else's. It doesn't stand out from all the other cars. That applies to a lot of things on the reservation.

"Kyle Goklish is like a new car. He's our best player and he's a great student, a first-rate kid and a great example for others. He's so good at running track that we've built our whole program around him. The basketball team needs him badly too, but I hear kids talking about him in school, and it amazes me. They call him a 'cheap player.' They say, 'He runs cheap, he plays ball cheap.' They'll say anything to bring him down to their level. I would have killed to be able to play sports like Kyle, but both the teenagers and some of the adults in Whiteriver talk this way about him. Everyone wants him to be a rescar and get dented like everyone else.

"It's the same thing with my number one chess player. They ridicule him, too."

The reality I was confronting in Whiteriver was more complex and subtle than I'd anticipated. The kids resisted change because, regardless of how difficult things might have been on the reservation, it remained, as people kept telling me, their home and comfort zone.

It was what they knew and had always known, and anything that was outside of that zone was potentially threatening and frightening. Life here was hard but familiar. Everything here was family to them, but that family ended when they got off their land.

*   *   *

AS A BOY growing up in Manhattan, I'd become fascinated with history after finding arrowheads, musket balls, and other military artifacts on Fort George Hill in Harlem, the site of battles in the Revolutionary War period in America. As I'd grown older, I'd become more and more interested in the nineteenth-century American West and had begun collecting art and other things from that era. A Buffalo Soldier uniform is on display in my den in L.A., and a battleshirt worn by a Commanche—collected by a Buffalo Soldier—hangs over the fireplace.

In the fall of 1998 I was encountering the past in a different and deeper way—my own past and the past of the kids I was attempting to coach. History was about more than which side won which skirmish at which location and on which date. It was about the legacy that is left behind in the lives of human beings and whether or not they are going to be restricted by the things their families had been restricted by or whether they are going to go forward and attempt something new.

I wasn't just trying to teach these kids basketball, but to penetrate and expand their comfort zone.

— XII —

YOU'RE NEVER SURE HOW A TEAM WILL PERFORM in a real game based on their practices. Our first test of the season came during Thanksgiving week. The Falcons had been invited to the St. Gregory's Tournament in Tuscon, about a four-hour drive in the big blue bus that carried the players and coaches all over east central Arizona. The team's rides to and from game were legendary. Some took four or five hours—one way—over winding mountain passes, dirt roads, and snow-covered asphalt. After finishing a varsity game at around 9:00 P.M., the team cleaned up and got back on the bus for the endless trip home, often traveling a couple hundred miles through bad weather before arriving back in Whiteriver at two or three in the morning. The next day at school, you could tell the players by the slump in their shoulders and the glazed look in their eyes.

The 180-mile journey to Tucson went over a high-country, narrow, two-lane highway and down into the bottom of Salt River Canyon, the lowest point on the reservation, at only 2,700 feet above sea level. It was a slow, winding, harrowing ride in a cold rainstorm, but the trip unfolded without any problems. The players spent their time joking with one another, talking about girls, snoozing, or putting on their headphones and listening to their current music of choice: rhythm and blues by R. Kelly or rap by singers like the late Tupac Shakur.

Throughout the season I occasionally rode the bus with the team and used these hours to get to know the guys better, to speak to them about their backgrounds and ambitions, substance abuse, and the value of getting more education. I strongly encouraged them to prepare themselves for college and think about life after their athletic days were finished. I pointed out the long odds against any high school athlete making money playing pro basketball. The bus trips were grueling yet worthwhile. In high school, college, or the NBA, teams really become teams when they travel together, and these journeys are good opportunities to loosen up and talk more openly, to make friends. I had to keep telling myself that the kids were getting to know me and my personality as much as I was getting to know them.

Tony Parker had made a comment in one of the articles written about my coaching the Falcons that had stayed with me. He'd said that I didn't know how to talk to the guys on the team or how to act around them at first, so they didn't quite know what to make of me. I had often wanted to speak more freely with them, but I'd kept quiet many times out of respect for their culture and way of playing the game. I was taking my time before opening my mouth and holding back because that was just my style.

WHEN THE SEASON BEGAN, I feared that some of the Falcons' bad habits in practice would emerge in the games. Coach Mendoza and I had never really been able to get the guys to slow down and work on their weaknesses. They'd kept resisting our advice, almost as if they wanted to prove us wrong—and to show us that they could win without our help. When we arrived in Tucson for the tournament, I was concerned about this, but I'd learned from my own coaches in grade school, high school, and college that sometimes the best way to teach young people to succeed is to let them try their own way for a while and fail.

We won three games and lost three in Tucson, but our last one of the tourney told the story. It contained everything we did badly and everything we did well, and it revealed the character of the team. It was also a classic game and a turning point for me because it was during this contest that I stopped holding back.

On a chilly, rainy Saturday afternoon, November 28, we played for fifth place against Cholla. It was a 4A school (Alchesay was 3A) and located in Tucson itself. Cholla had 1,600 high school students, more than twice as many as Alchesay. For weeks, we'd been telling our kids that they could beat teams worse than themselves by playing run-and-gun basketball, but that wouldn't mean very much as the season progressed. The important games would come when we played squads more talented than ours. Then, in order to win, we would have to lay aside one-on-one basketball and work together as a team.

Cholla had more height than we did and probably better players. They had a little more of everything, except for one thing. As Rick Sanchez had been telling me since I'd arrived in Whiteriver, Alchesay High had the best fans in basketball. I didn't believe him until I saw how many Falcon supporters had driven four hours over tough roads and through rainy weather to get to the St. Gregory gym. We had more fans in the stands than Cholla did—and ours were louder.

During the warm-up before the Cholla contest, I was sitting on our bench going over some notes I had made for our game plan. I was very absorbed and did not notice the approach of a small boy named Cedric, age four, who was the nephew of one of our players. Cedric nonchalantly came right up to me and sat down on my lap, leaning over my leg to see what I was reading. All this was so carefree and natural that I just let it happen. He seemed more like my own nephew at this point, and once again this brought home my sense of being accepted by the White Mountain tribe. A real bonus.

The Cholla game started the way our other tournament games had. We fell behind because of our constant mistakes, the same mistakes the guys had been making day after day in practice: throwing the ball away, putting up poor shots, missing layups, not blocking out and getting rebounds, not playing under control. We got behind because we didn't execute the way Coach Mendoza and I had told them to during the past few weeks.

But when we got far enough behind, something happened— something that seemed to be at the root of the team's identity. Call it the *Mission Impossible* factor. Once we got down so far that the game began to look helpless, the Falcons suddenly woke up and started to play harder, as if they could only be motivated by sensing that they were going to lose. This was maddening for the coaching staff. Mendoza, Rick Sanchez, Tommy Parker, and I sat on the bench together and glared at them, but that didn't do much good. At the end of the first quarter, we trailed 20–11, and it looked like a blowout for Cholla.

In the second quarter, Ivan Lamkin, our "Big Sexy" substitute center, entered the game and steadied the team. He wasn't a good practice player—he complained a lot about minor injuries and not having the time to put in the work we'd asked of him, or he made other excuses about what he couldn't get done. Yet sometimes when we put him into a game, he came to life and looked dominant for several minutes—blocking shots, grabbing rebounds, and even scoring. When he did something well, he began to glow with pride, but he also seemed to stop and listen to the applause of the crowd as it floated down on him. Not a good thing to do in a sport as fast as basketball.

Ivan briefly took over and changed the flow of the game, turning it against the taller Cholla kids. The other Falcons picked up on this, and Alchesay pulled to within three points before Cholla made another run and went into the half leading 31–23.

It looked like a routine loss for us, the kind of game I had already come to expect from the team. We played hard and put out for the thirty-two minutes of the contest, but we simply couldn't win the tough ones without changing our ways. Everything I'd seen and felt about our players was bearing itself out on the court.

Too many athletes, at every level of sports, believe they can triumph on their talent alone and don't need to learn new things. They're simply wrong. (When I was well into my thirties, NBA consultant and teacher Pete Newell showed me how to use my arms better so that I could fend off opponents and get more rebounds; this almost immediately improved my performance.) The best players are the ones who constantly go in search of knowledge and never stop seeking it—at least until their bodies start to give out. You have to be humbled to understand all this, and the Falcons hadn't gotten there yet.

In the locker room during the half, as Coach Mendoza reminded them to settle down on the floor and handle the ball better, I sat silently and observed, not having much to say that I hadn't already said many times before in practice. When Mendoza finished, Rusty Taylor did what he always did during games: He kept statistics and with great enthusiasm he now rattled them off to the players and staff, telling us which Cholla player was hot and needed to be stopped, how many rebounds we had versus the other team, and how well we were shooting the ball.

The kids sat on wooden benches and drank water from plastic bottles. They dripped sweat through their yellow uniforms with blue trim, gazing up at us with the same look they always wore—polite attention, as if they were absorbing every word we said. They used this expression with adults, I was beginning to think, mostly in order to satisfy us that they were listening.

When Taylor was finished, Mendoza asked me if I had anything to add. I briefly repeated some of what had already been talked about, telling them to tighten up on defense and use their bodies to keep the other team away from the basket. Then Butter stood and brought all the guys together in the middle of the locker room. They bent over and put their hands on top of one another's.

"All right!" Butter said, leading them into the ritual.

"All right!" the other boys echoed.

Pumping their hands and shoulders, they yelled in their deepest and most powerful voices, "One, two, three, Falcons!"

They cheered and clapped and ran back onto the court for the warm-ups before the start of the second half. I followed them out of the locker room, walking beside the other coaches and watching our kids shoot baskets.

I had enjoyed coming to Whiteriver and working with the team, but so far I had mostly stayed outside of the experience. I hadn't made any big speeches or shown much emotion with the players. I hadn't gotten caught up in the hoopla that surrounds sporting events, even in high school. I'd laid back and watched things, trying to remember what it was like to be a minority teenager and how I'd wanted to be handled when I was their age. I hadn't wanted to intrude too much and definitely did not want to become the center of attention.

But games are powerful and unpredictable things. We like them for many reasons, and some of us seem to need them to help us release certain feelings. We also like them because there is no script, no known outcome, and they can spontaneously pull us into their drama and shake us and touch us in some very basic ways—as I was about to find out.

— XIII —

THE THIRD QUARTER WENT ALONG IN THE SAME pattern as the first two. We kept running and making mistakes, while Cholla kept increasing its lead. Going into the final eight minutes, they were ahead 52–40, and there had been no indication of what was to come, no hint that I was about to see—and hear—my first real demonstration of Apache basketball.

The taller and more athletic Cholla players now began showing signs of tiredness. As they did, Tony and Kyle and Loren started stealing the ball from them and taking it up the court for a score. They found another gear and were suddenly all over the Cholla guards, playing more physically than they ever had in practice, harassing them with their hands and knees and chests, executing nasty but legal defense, diving for every loose ball on the floor, then grabbing it and dashing down the floor for two more points.

The rest of our guys—Brennen and Ivan and Tinker and Willie and Blaine—caught the wave of this energy and began playing more fiercely. They ran and bumped and scrapped; they jumped and scrambled and pressed their opponents from one end of the court to the other. They played with total abandon, as if this were what they had been waiting to do all along, and now they had their chance. Something was coming out of them, something that had been buried up to this point, and it seemed unstoppable.

A wild movement was unfolding in front of me, a whirl of arms and legs in motion. The fire that I'd seen that first day in practice, when they were dashing hell-bent through the three-on-three drills, now flared again, except this time they were involved in a real game and struggling to catch up. There was purpose in what they were doing—and there were results. They were playing so hard that Cholla was soon flustered and their offense began breaking down on the court, making mistakes of their own.

Our fans, who were mostly gathered behind the bench where I was sitting, hadn't had much to cheer about this afternoon. But when they saw and felt what was happening on the floor, they responded with screams that grew louder with each steal and each basket the Falcons made. The score was getting closer and the bleachers in St. Gregory's gym were starting to shake. Our fans shouted and stomped their feet the way fans do everywhere. But then they did something else, something I had never heard during a game, so it took me a few moments to recognize the sound. They sent out war cries—high-pitched, chilling, piercing Apache war cries so penetrating that they caused me to turn around and stare at where they were coming from. They made the skin twitch on the back of my neck.

We had forced Cholla into one turnover, then another, and then another. We made up nine points very fast. The score was 56–53 with four minutes left. All the players and coaches on our bench were standing up and watching, and I was standing with them, waving my arms and making my own noise.

Our cheerleaders—seven young women and a mascot named

Josh, who was dressed in street clothes because he was still waiting for his Falcon costume to be finished—were leading the crowd through timeworn Alchesay routines. The girls were leaping, and Josh was flushed from exertion.

I was shouting to Kyle and Tony to keep it up. Rick Sanchez and Tommy Parker were standing beside me, yelling their own advice. I looked over at them, and we exchanged grins, as if they were glad to see me up and screaming. I had forgotten my usual restraint and was falling further and further into the pull of Apache basketball. When our guys went for another steal, I did something I'd never planned on doing, but the heat of the game had brought its spell down on me.

A referee made a terrible call—blowing his whistle for a foul against us—just as we were about to swipe the ball again. I was never one to let a bad call go, so I whipped off my glasses and stuck them out at the official, letting him know that he needed help with his vision.

This kind of thing is commonplace at the pro level, where the banter between players and refs gets very intimate, but not at a high school game. Offering my glasses was going too far in this setting, but it was too late to rethink my strategy.

The ref walked up to me and my glasses were dangling right in front of his nose. He stopped cold and stared at me. It was not a pretty expression. I'd clearly taken him by surprise (and myself by surprise, too). I hadn't meant to embarrass him, but right now that was the way he looked.

He raised his hands in front of him, and I felt bad, because I was certain that he was going to shape them into a "T." That would have signaled a technical foul against me, which would have given Cholla two free throws plus another possession of the ball. That could have hurt our team and even affected the final score.

When I realized what I'd done and just how far into the game I'd gotten, I started to go back to the huddle, wondering what his next move would be.

He glared at me and bit down on his whistle but did not blow it. He lowered his hands and walked off. I sat down and shook my head, relieved that the moment had passed.

I glanced over at Rick and Tommy, who were sitting next to me. They were laughing nervously.

"Man," Rick said, "I thought he was going to T you up, Kareem."

"That was close," Tommy said with a big smile.

"Yeah." I nodded. "Too close."

They both grinned at me, as if to say, "Now you see why people get excited at Falcons games."

We went back to watching the action on the floor, but soon we were up and yelling again. Our team didn't play the best basketball, but when their game kicked in and the blood started to flow and they made their opponent falter, when our fans rose to their feet and began to holler with cries that bounced around the gym and made you shiver, you could feel why the Falcons liked doing things their way. It was chaotic but incredibly exciting.

I'd never been this worked up over a game in the 1990s. The decade of pro basketball since my retirement had not moved me nearly as much as the previous one had. Of course, I'd been a player in the 1980s, so maybe I wasn't objective, but those battles that the Lakers had had with Philadelphia, Boston, and Detroit had been great athletic dramas, no matter who you were rooting for. You never knew who was going to win. We'd beaten each of those teams for a title and they'd all beaten us. The 1990s had been too dominated by one team, the Chicago Bulls, and one player, Michael Jordan.

The Bulls were good, but their competition was not what ours had been. (The 1985 Lakers would have taken them in a championship series.) I believed that the game had suffered because of a lack of teams that could really challenge the Bulls. The single matchup I would have most liked to see in the 1990s—Jordan's Bulls versus Hakeem Olajuwon's Houston Rockets—never happened. So my involvement as a fan had lessened. The only basketball I'd really watched was my son Kareem at Western Kentucky. He'd been a starting forward and an academic all-American.

Now my passion was coming back, even though I was an assistant coach on a high school team instead of a pro player. I was starting to care again about a group of guys, even though they were prep players rather than NBA all-stars. They were letting me feel my old attachment to the game I loved, letting me lose myself in the competition. I was teaching them some new techniques, but they were stirring my emotions and making me stand up and cheer.

Pro fans may have been feeling alienated because the NBA was on strike, but these kids were giving the game back to me. I was catching my old basketball fever, and it felt good.

THE GAME MOVED back and forth; Cholla made a basket, and we did, too. They made another and I shouted for our guys to play tougher defense and stop Cholla on each possession. All of our coaching strategy had been laid aside. We weren't doing anything we'd outlined in practice, but working as hard as we could and playing to win. Kyle stole the ball and took it in for a layup. Then Tony did the same. With 1:26 left, we were down 64–63, and the gym was so loud you could barely hear the refs' whistle.

Butter made a foul shot to tie the game. We got the ball again with less than a minute to go—and the chance to pull ahead for the first time. But we missed and Cholla rebounded with fourteen seconds left. We fouled them, but their free throws bounced off the rim and we got the ball back. Tony drove down the floor and fired up one last shot at the buzzer. As it sailed toward the basket, everybody in the gym craned a neck to follow the flight of the ball and see if it would fall through the net. It clanked off the backboard as the horn sounded.

The game was over. Time had run out, and the score was still tied.

After all that effort had been expended on the floor by both teams, nothing had been settled. It was a truly unsatisfying ending.

The gym had gone dead silent. Nobody had wanted the game to conclude like this. The refs walked to the center of the court and huddled together while the crowd looked on and waited, hoping the officials would let it go into overtime.

The championship game of the St. Gregory tournament was scheduled for later that evening. Usually high school referees did not allow a consolation game like ours to go beyond four quarters, because it really didn't matter who won fifth place. But this game was different. It had become special, and everyone, including the refs, could sense that.

As they stood together and discussed the situation, the kids and the coaches looked at them with eyes that were pleading to let the game go on.

"Keep playing!" a fan behind me yelled.

"Don't stop!" said another.

The refs walked over to the scorers' table and announced that the game would continue with one four-minute overtime in order to decide the winner. Players on both sides broke into smiles, and the crowd erupted with pleasure.

THE ACTION RESUMED AND IT WAS EXACTLY AS before—one basket for us and one for Cholla. Neither team could pull away. They were a better squad, but we were undaunted in our will to keep up with them. None of the casual attitude I'd seen among our players at practice was evident now. Tony and Kyle and Brennen were absolutely focused on the court. They were drenched with perspiration—Tony's jersey was hanging out of his pants and he kept using it to wipe his face. He was constantly talking on the floor: to his teammates, his opponents, and himself. During time-outs, he talked in the huddle when the coaches were trying to make a point.

Now more than ever, the faces of the young men looked like the old pictures of Apache warriors, except these kids were wearing soaked uniforms and tennis shoes. Their muscles were glistening and their chests heaving. Their faces had the glow that comes from extreme effort, and their cheekbones looked higher than ever. They wanted this game badly; they wanted to beat this big-city team from Tucson. If we lost, the coaching staff could criticize them for many things, but not for lack of effort.

With a minute left in overtime, the score was tied again. Cholla made a basket and went up by two. Kyle drove the ball hard upcourt with ten seconds to go. He shot and missed, but was fouled with two seconds remaining on the clock. With our fans falling silent and Cholla's fans screaming for him to fail, he bounced the ball a couple of bounces at the free throw line and made the first shot. Our crowd exhaled and exploded into cheers. He paused and dribbled at the line again, eying the basket and raising the ball to his chin. He launched it in an arc, sending it cleanly through the net.

Cholla quickly threw the ball in, but time ran out with the score 73–73 and the game still not decided.

As our players wandered over to the bench, looking both disappointed and hopeful, the refs went to center court for another conference. What should they do now? Call the game and send the teams home or keep playing until the tie was finally broken? The crowd was standing. Everyone was watching the referees, pointing at them and demanding that they let the game go on.

Coach Mendoza and I smiled at each other. Then all of the coaches traded smiles. Games like this were one reason we'd orginally gotten involved in the sport and why we kept coming back to it even though we were no longer kids.

"You like this?" Rick asked me.

"Yeah," I said.

"Pretty good game," Tommy said.

"Yeah," I said again.

Basketball can do that to you. It can give you an indefinable sense of hope and joy. Those things were on full display on this cool, gloomy, rainy afternoon in late November in Tucson. After four quarters and one overtime of play, nobody knew what was going to happen next, and everyone in the gym cared.

Sometimes an athletic event takes on a life of its own and becomes more interesting than anyone engaged in it. Regardless of what's at stake or for whom you're cheering—or even if you're a referee and aren't rooting for either team—you want a clear-cut outcome. That feeling gnaws at your chest, even if the game is just for fifth place in a preseason tourney in front of a few hundred people. You want the drama to continue; you want some kind of resolution. Otherwise, the game loses its meaning.

After consulting for a few seconds, the refs went back to the scorers' table and said that another overtime would be allowed.

The game went forward and, amazingly, the pattern repeated itself. Neither team would budge. The score was tied at 75 and then 77. Both squads now looked exhausted. Our kids, especially the bigger ones, were dragging themselves up and down the court, bent over at the knees and searching for air. Cholla's kids were equally beat. Yet they all kept playing as hard as they could. I was proud of our guys for putting up this kind of fight. I was proud of both teams.

We finally went ahead for the first time, 79–77, and it looked as if the Falcons would hold on and get the win. But Cholla came back to tie it at 79 and then both teams stalled. The second overtime ended in another deadlock.

By now, even the crowd was drained, yet the war cries kept coming from behind our bench, not quite as loudly as before. Our cheerleaders were also looking tired, but doing their best to keep up an ear-shattering teenage din. When the refs went to center court once more, you knew they were not going to stop the action now and send the teams home tied. We'd all come too far for that. Sooner or later, something had to give.

The third overtime commenced and, mustering all the energy they had left, the two teams went at it again. We threw the ball away three times in a row, our old bad habits catching up with us at last. Cholla took advantage of our mistakes. They went ahead 86–85, then ran off five straight points. The Falcons could not start another rally. At the very end, we were still scrambling, but the clock ran out and the endless game was over. Cholla was victorious, 94–87.

As I walked off the court, I passed a Cholla coach and heard him saying something to one of the assistants, a remark that would be a factor throughout the Falcons' season. "We beat Kareem's team," he said. "We did it. We beat Kareem Abdul-Jabbar."

In coming to Alchesay, I knew that I might be putting more pressure on the kids because other schools would want to boast not just that they beat last year's runner-up in the state 3A tournament, but that they beat the team I was coaching. I realized this might make us a marked squad, but after watching this afternoon's game, I stopped worrying about it. All sports are about dealing with pressure and being able to perform in front of other people when it counts. The sooner an athlete gets used to that, the better. Besides, the Falcons seemed to play best under pressure; the real challenge for the coaches was getting them to play well before they fell so far behind and had to fight to get back into the game.

After shaking hands with their opponents, our guys went into the locker room and I followed behind them. I had mixed feelings about what I'd just seen. I was proud of the kids for playing so hard, but as they sat in front of their lockers and shook their heads in disappointment, I told them that if they would listen to the coaches in practice and work on their fundamentals, they would make a lot fewer mistakes and wouldn't need these frantic fourth-quarter comebacks that often ended in defeat. They wouldn't have to push themselves to the point of collapse and then lose in overtime. They could get ahead and force the other team to chase them.

They nodded at my remarks, but were clearly discouraged.

As I rode home that night from Tucson, I decided that it had been a good loss for us, potentially a good learning experience. The game had shown us that we could beat mediocre teams by running them into the floor, but when we reached the important tournaments in February, we would be quickly eliminated unless we did some things differently. The Cholla game could be a pivotal moment for the Falcons. The guys had done things their way on the court at St. Gregory's, and the result was an exhausting loss. Maybe now they would be more willing to pay attention to what the coaches had been trying to tell them for a month.

I would talk about all this with them on Monday afternoon at our next practice, but would they listen?

— XV —

THAT MONDAY, NOVEMBER 30, I WAS INVITED to the Fifth Annual Apache Women's Conference, held at the Hon Dah Casino, nineteen miles north of Whiteriver. FATCO and the casino are the major Apache-owned-and-operated employers of Native Americans on the reservation. The money generated from the casino is not shared with individual tribal members, as in some Indian communities, but goes into a general fund for education, building, and other projects. Income from businesses and properties on the reservation is not taxed by the state of Arizona but is taxed by the federal government.

The Hon Dah Casino opened at the end of 1997 and has 152 full-time workers, servicing both the casino itself and the 128-room luxury hotel connected to it. The casino offers penny, nickel, quarter, dollar, and five-dollar slot machines, live poker, bingo, video blackjack, video poker, and video keno. It provides lodging for the gamblers and the bear, elk, and other big-game hunters who visit the area each fall. In late November, you can see the hunters leaving the hotel early in the morning wearing their camouflage clothing and heavy boots, with their long-barreled guns flung over their shoulders.

The casino never closes and is always full of action. At six-thirty in the morning, when the sky was still dark and the air biting cold, causing frost to streak the car windows in the casino parking lot, Apache men and women sat at the slot machines inside the Hon Dah, smoking cigarettes and playing nickels and quarters. Some of the gamblers were staying in the hotel and had just gotten up. Some were on their way to work at construction jobs and had stopped by to get warm, have a cup of coffee, and test their luck. Some hadn't yet gone to bed. Ashtrays and rows of coins were stacked in front of them and they reached down and dropped the money into the machines, one coin after the other, repeating the process over and over again. The machines whirled and usually came up blank, so the gamblers dropped more money into the slots and hoped their fortunes would change.

Guards constantly patroled the casino aisles, checking everyone out, looking for cheaters, pickpockets, and other undesirables. Bright lights flashed from the ceiling, splashing green or red or blue rays down onto the gamblers' faces. Overhead, loud music was continually piped in, holiday music, like a country-and-western singer crooning "Rudolph, the Red-Nosed Reindeer." A ventilation system was churning, but smoke was everywhere.

On the walls of the cashiers' office were handsome black-and-white photos of long-dead Apache men and women, some of them performing ancient rituals and others staring into the camera with their rifles held across their forearms. They looked weathered and hard and able to survive almost anything. They looked lean, healthy, alert, brave—and totally foreign in this casino setting. Everything about the place—from the gambling to the sensory overstimulation to the overabundance of food they served you in the adjoining restaurant to the over-solicitous service the waitresses provided as you ate—represented comfort and security and affluence, a good and easy way of life. The casino has added color, jobs, and entertainment to this quiet corner of Arizona, but the goings-on at the Hon Dah always seemed rather unreal compared to the pictures of those Apache ancestors staring down at you from the walls. They looked more alive than the gamblers.

Casinos are strange places full of strange feelings. The first time I visited this one, an older woman, perhaps seventy, came up to me, fell to the carpet, wrapped her arms around my legs, and begged me for an autograph. I was embarrassed for her, but she kept begging and would not stand up. I told her I would give her what she wanted if she got off the floor and stopped behaving like that, so she did.

At all hours of the day or night, a steady flow of people came into the casino and took their seats in front of the machines, as the lights beamed, the music blared, and the video gambling games made those odd bouncing noises that sound like a computer going crazy. All the elements inside the Hon Dah—the Apache history, the Apache present, the canned Christmas songs, the overweight gamblers, and the walls of smoke—intermingled with one another, perfectly reflecting how Native Americans have tried to adapt to modern times and compete with the rest of the world. The Hon Dah has been good to the local people and given them much, but it's a very long way from their old way of life. You couldn't help wondering that if something had been gained in the past few years, something else was being lost.

THAT OLDER WAY OF LIFE was evoked by the women attending the conference at the hotel. Many showed up wearing traditional clothing: long turquoise dresses worn with black leather belts studded with silver ornaments; flowing print skirts worn with high boots or low-cut moccasins. Others wore full-length pink, green, dark blue, or purple dresses with diamond shapes sewn onto the hems. They pulled their shining black hair back in ponytails.

The women were mostly short and heavy-set. They looked strong and enduring and deeply rooted in this part of the earth, conjuring up a stand of old trees. Aging women with gray hair limped into the lobby of the casino and gazed around at the permanent displays designed to evoke the Old West. Here were fake black bears and fake mountain lions climbing on fake trunks and fake branches. The women seemed surprised at finding themselves in this fancy but artificial setting. Their expressions were full of wonder, as if they had lived through a couple of centuries' worth of historical change in the past few decades. Yet they seemed eager to participate in the conference and curious about the future of the reservation.

During the luncheon, the women asked me to speak, and I got a bashful attack. I hadn't prepared anything to say and was tongue-tied for several moments. Then I thanked them in Apache for inviting me and told them that they were beautiful, also remembering the Apache word for pretty, which is *denzoni.* I said that I would do my best in coaching their sons and grandsons and nephews and cousins.

The women were extemely friendly to me and didn't appear to be used to this kind of attention. They acted as if they couldn't quite believe that an outsider would want to come live and work with them. I enjoyed their company and would have liked to stay longer at the luncheon, but after eating I excused myself and drove down to Whiteriver to get ready for practice.

This would be our most important workout to date, and before it started I wanted the chance to mull over what I was going to say to the team. I wanted to do what my coaches had done for me when they'd passed down their hard-won knowledge to myself and other young players. After I'd gotten older and looked back at what they had given me I felt a strong satisfaction about that process. I had been part of a great learning process, a tradition that had started long before I was born.

I wanted to carry on that tradition. The Falcons had lost a game they had deeply wanted to win—and they'd had the opportunity to think about their three-overtime defeat to Cholla during the four-hour bus ride back to Whiteriver and throughout the past weekend. Maybe this afternoon, they would finally be in a listening mood. Maybe they were ready to leave their comfort zone, and maybe it was time for me to set some boundaries and establish some consequences. From now on, anyone making a bad pass in practice owed the team some push-ups.

I ASKED THE GUYS to sit on the floor in a semi-circle in front of me and to help each other stretch, pulling on one another's arms and legs, loosening up their back and shoulder muscles.

As they did this, I lay on the court and did some yoga exercises. Yoga had helped me from sustaining serious injuries throughout most of my career.

A few minutes earlier, Coach Mendoza had told me that neither Butter nor Ivan would be traveling with us to the town of

Pinon for our next game, two nights from now. They'd been caught "passing snuff" at school and had been suspended for one game. Just because the kids didn't drink or take drugs or smoke (at least they hadn't been caught doing any of these things so far) didn't mean they weren't willing to try another stimulant like chewing tobacco. There was always another temptation on the horizon.

Brennen and Ivan weren't quite ready to make a commitment to the team. Neither was Tony Parker, our second best player after Kyle, who had continued doing things his way on the court, running and gunning and sometimes playing out of control. He'd also talked when the coaches were giving instructions at practice or during time-outs at games. Dealing with this distraction was a waste of time. It was almost December and enough time had already been wasted.

Mendoza stood before the guys and patiently explained to them that they needed to become more serious about basketball and watch more videos of our games. (The contests were broadcast live on the radio and were also taped for study later on by the coaching staff and players.) He wanted the kids to spend time breaking down the film and seeing what they needed to work on.

Mendoza's remarks were brief, and after finishing up, he asked if I had something to say. I rose and looked down at the guys scattered across the shiny hardwood floor. They looked very young just now and again reminded me of myself at their age. They surely had a lot of confusion and mixed emotions about many things, including their racial background. They probably had anger over this issue, as I had had as a teenager, but it hadn't yet coalesced into anything meaningful inside of them. They were still just kids trying to figure out who they were and carve out an identity.

I was gradually getting to know more about them and their families—and about what they were contending with at home. Some had two solid parents, but others had absent fathers, over-stressed single mothers, alcoholic relatives, and flare-ups of violence between the adults in the household. They were dealing with many other invisible things from the tribe's past.

From reading and talking with local people, I knew that Apache boys were particularly sensitive to criticism and often reacted badly to it. While growing up, they tended to be pampered and treated as special when compared with the young girls. This was a carryover from their ancient history, when males had been trained to be the protectors of the tribe—the warriors—and females were expected to manage the day-to-day details of running their families and getting things done. Boys were seen as special; without them, the tribe would not survive. The boys had to hunt, fight their enemies, and face death. Because of this, they were spoiled and even given to understand that they could do no wrong. As a result, girls tended to become more responsible and more pragmatic, more realistic about themselves and more grounded at a much earlier age. The society had long been matrilineal. Women, in one form or another, basically ran the show.

Such conditions, according to some observers of the White Mountain Apache, still applied. I was encountering these ghosts as I stood to address the team.

I wanted to be gentle but firm. I wanted to be critical but didn't want the criticism to become too personal. So for a while, I directed my remarks at the whole group.

"I need to know," I told them, "what you guys want to do with the rest of the season. We can make a decision right now and get this thing settled. We don't need to waste our time or your time at practice. If you just want to run up and down the court and throw the ball away and put up wild shots, we can do that. You've already proven you're good at that. That will be our year and our experience together. That will be what you take away from this.

"But if you want to keep growing and playing better basketball, we can do that, too, but we need to make some changes. Some of you have the talent to go on and play the game at a higher level, but you'll never do that unless you decide to work on your fundamentals. At the next level, there's always going to be someone with more talent than you. Always. And if you haven't gotten rid of your weaknesses and built on your strengths, you're going to get left behind. The choice is yours.

"If you want to keep shooting the ball wrong and sending it off your palms instead of your fingers, the choice is yours. If you want to keep flying out of control, the choice is yours. If you want to keep jumping up in the air with the ball before you have any idea what you're going to do next—and then being forced into making a bad pass—the choice is yours. We can't help you if you aren't willing to help yourselves. But if you want to improve and will make a commitment to that process, that choice is yours, too."

I paused and let my words settle in for a few seconds. Then I stared down at Tony, who was lying on the floor on his side with his head propped up by his hand. He hadn't been listening to me and was looking around the gym as if he were daydreaming. I didn't speak until his eyes wandered up to meet mine.

"Tony," I said.

His head jerked to attention.

"Do you and I have a problem?"

His eyes got bigger, but he didn't say anything.

"You like to talk when we're trying to coach. That doesn't work. Do we have a problem?"

He barely shook his head.

"If we have a problem, we need to work it out now. Do we have a problem?"

"No," he said softly. His cheeks were flushed. He had just been singled out from the group and would not forget it.

"Are you sure we don't have a problem?"

He nodded.

"Okay, guys," I said, addressing all of them again. "Let's get to work."

SOMETHING HAPPENED after my little talk on that last afternoon in November—just as something happened a few days later when I stopped practice after Tinker threw the ball away, as he'd been doing since the season began. Coach Mendoza had never responded to these mistakes in any concrete way; he'd just spoken a few sentences, which had evaporated a couple of seconds later in the sweaty gym air. Then Tinker had gone back to tossing the ball away.

I believed in the concrete example. People don't learn by being allowed to get away with things. They learn by what they remember. On this occasion, after Tinker had fired the ball out of bounds, I told him to hit the floor and give me twenty push-ups. Each time he made a miscue with the ball, I said, I wanted him to repeat this process. The same thing would apply to everyone.

As his teammates looked on, Tinker got down and did the push-ups. None of them had ever been disciplined this way by Coach Mendoza and they seemed surprised, if not shocked, that someone would hold them accountable in this manner.

The kids needed their expectations rattled. They needed to see that their actions on and off the court had consequences. After Tinker did the push-ups, his passing slowly got better and the rest of the team began to practice more seriously.

Collection of Kareem Abdul-Jabbar; photograph by Wen Roberts

TOP: 1863 Sharps carbine conversion, Company K, Ninth Cavalry.
BOTTOM LEFT: 1860 "Bummer" forage cap stamped B Company, Ninth Cavalry
roster #27. Records show trooper #27 to be one Private Dennis Johnson.
BOTTOM RIGHT: Ninth Cavalry canteen.

Collection of Kareem Abdul-Jabbar; photograph by Wen Roberts

TOP CENTER: 1885 campaign hat, Tenth Cavalry.
BOTTOM: Campaign belt from L. Company, Tenth Cavalry.
TOP RIGHT: Spurs issued A Company, Tenth Cavalry.
TOP LEFT: 1860 Colt Army revolver issued to F Company, Tenth Cavalry.

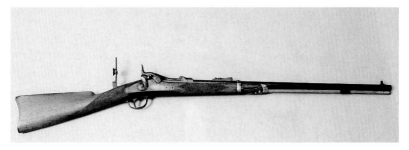

Collection of Kareem Abdul-Jabbar; photograph by Wen Roberts

First type 1875 officer's model Springfield rifle that belonged to
Lieutenant Charles Gatewood.

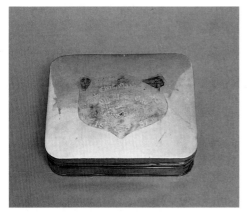

Silver jewelry case presented to Lieutenant Gatewood by the troops, inscribed "Lt. Chas. Gatewood 6th U.S. Cav. 1887." Lieutenant Gatewood is the person who successfully asked Geronimo to surrender. He spent many days in the field with elements of the Ninth and Tenth Cavalry in his capacity as the officer in charge of the Apache scouts from San Carlos and Fort Apache. He is buried in Arlington Cemetery. The case contains his shoulder knots and collar bars (shown below).

Collection of Kareem Abdul-Jabbar; photograph by Wen Roberts

Collection of Kareem Abdul-Jabbar; photograph by Wen Roberts

Lieutenant
Charles B. Gatewood.

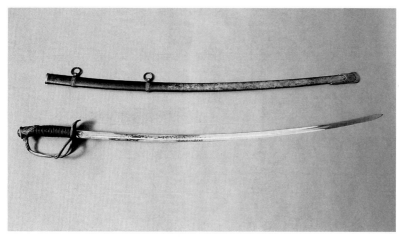

1872 Cavalry officer's sword belonging to Lieutenant Phillip Bettens, Ninth Cavalry (West Point Class of 1885). Lieutenant Bettens led troops in the fight at Drexel Mission one day after the battle at Wounded Knee.

Mystery photograph of
John T. Glass with the White
Mountain Apache Scouts.

Arizona Historical Society/Tucson AHS #50140

My photograph of John T. Glass.

Collection of Kareem Abdul-Jabbar

— XVI —

SOME DAYS, SUPERINTENDENT JOHN CLARK SHOWED up for practice. He usually had a smile on his face, and it was always good to see him come strolling through the gym door. He liked to stand on the sidelines and joke around with the players and coaches. He reminded me of a big, balding teenager who loved to hang out with his friends and have fun. He'd been known to slip away from his office at lunchtime and go trout fishing, but he was also very committed to his job. Even though he'd been at Alchesay for the past six years and oversaw the entire White Mountain Apache school system, he still regarded himself as an outsider on the reservation. That system included three elementary schools, one middle school, and one high school, with a total of more than 2,500 students.

A Vietnam veteran with four kids of his own, Clark had grown up near the Grand Canyon and had been a teacher in Whiteriver back in the 1970s. He'd soon become enthralled with the place— with the landscape and the Native Americans who had inhabited it for centuries. In the nineties, he came back as superintendent, but now lived off the reservation. When he spoke about his work, he conveyed a lot of affection and respect for the local people.

"I don't have a home in Whiteriver," he said, "because, first of all, the town is just for the White Mountain Apache population. And second, there is such a housing shortage here that to take one away from someone else would be ridiculous."

After returning to Whiteriver as superintendent, he noticed when walking across the playgrounds or through the school hallways that virtually none of the youngsters was speaking Apache. That told him that the old language was dying off, and not just inside the school but at home. Having one's own language, he knew from his educational background, was critical to a people's sense of history, identity, and self-esteem.

"Until very recently," he said, "the use of the Apache language was discouraged in our school system, and the kids were punished for using it. Since I've been here, I've tried to change this. Our school board is made up of five elected tribal members, and we conduct our meetings in both English and Apache. I can't speak Apache myself, and if you try to do that without knowing how, it's very easy to make mistakes and insult someone. I had an administrator here once who attempted to greet a school board member in Apache. Instead of saying good morning, he ended up calling him a 'devil man.' You have to be careful about that.

"There's a conversational Apache and a higher level of the langauge that involves using place names and long pauses in your speech, which convey different meanings. It's different from anything in English and is a very sophisticated way of communicating. Back in the seventies, we had teacher aides at the school to translate what the kids were saying to the instructors, but now we have Apache-language aides who are teaching Apache to the kids. Edgar Perry gets a lot of credit for this. He's our on-site certified Apache teacher, and he's put together an Apache dictionary, which we're using in the classroom. Through all of these things, we're doing language maintenance. We're sending the message to our students that it's all right to speak Apache now, both at school and at home."

Clark has instituted a college undergraduate program at Alchesay, which encourages the school's secretaries or other personnel to attend higher education classes and pursue college degrees. One goal is to help them become teachers who will return to the reservation and go to work. In 1999, only 14 out of 163 teachers in the local school system were Native American, but Clark hoped to double that figure in the next few years.

"We're trying to change the whole educational environment," he said, "but frankly, it's tough. Kids don't see their parents reading, and reading is the key to academic success. There aren't a lot of role models here for that kind of success, just because formal education is still relatively new in the Apache culture. The role models here tend to be non–Native Americans, so that's why we're concentrating on bringing in more Native American teachers. A teacher here starts at $23,000 and can work up to $43,000 with a master's degree. That's a lot of money on the reservation, so teachers have status.

"People like myself, who are not Native American, are really just short-term visitors here. We need to prepare the local population to run the system after we're gone. The biggest challenge we face is not to go with the status quo, but to find new ways of doing things and reaching the students.

"We've got great kids here. That's the important thing to remember. They have a lot of things to overcome and they're heroes for just showing up at school each day. Many of them don't have two parents, but aunts and uncles help raise them. Family is the ray of hope on the reservation. Without such strong family bonds, the situtation would be bleak. If you were in trouble here or your car broke down or you needed a meal, half a dozen people would open up their wallets to you. The Apache have a very giving nature. That's one of the reasons I'm working here.

"Most Americans now have their families scattered all across the United States, but the Apache are centered here; they're very attached to the land. It's part of them and has meaning for them that it doesn't for people in most other places. I've heard stories of tribal leaders telling kids that if they're having problems with alcohol or drugs or a personal issue or a family member, they should go out and listen to the land. Sit with it and receive from it what it has to offer.

"The land is theirs. It belongs to them, and it will protect them, if they protect it. If they become silent and hear what the land has to tell them, they will be healed."

— XVII —

OUR FIRST THREE REGULAR SEASON GAMES were away from Whiteriver. We beat Pinon and Winslow before losing to Snowflake. The Winslow game began as a reversal of our pattern at the Tucson tournament. We got ahead early on, then lost our focus and blew a big lead, but held on to win our first good road victory of the year. That made the postgame pizza taste a lot better and the two-and-a-half-hour ride home in the middle of the night almost tolerable.

The Snowflake game, on the other hand, was a crusher. (This opponent would haunt us all year long.) We reverted to making too many turnovers and threw the game away. The real frustrations of coaching—of sitting and watching the action instead of being able to get on the court and do something to change the situation—sank in for the first time during this contest. I hadn't gotten used to sitting on the bench and would feel this frustration the rest of the season. Sometimes, I reached up to pull my hair and didn't find any.

Overall, we were playing more under control than we had in Tucson and were slowly improving. My November 30 talk at practice had accomplished something. We were starting to run the set plays we worked on every afternoon in the gym—and starting to get the ball inside to our bigger guys. We were bringing Ivan and Willie more into the game. We were gradually changing, yet flowing beneath the surface of our season was the basic conflict that had been there from the day I arrived. The coaches were trying to get the kids to slow down and break old habits and attempt something new. The players were interested in winning the best way (or the only way) they knew how. The fate of our season would revolve around this conflict.

MANY OF OUR FANS attended the first three away games, but I didn't get the full effect of Alchesay High basketball until we began playing at home in mid-December. From the seventeenth to the nineteenth, the school held its own tournament at the activity center. Watching us win three straight games and capture the tourney was gratifying. Even though our opponents weren't very strong, I was starting to think that we were making real progress.

An unfortunate incident occurred during the tournament, however, when we played archrival San Carlos, another Apache community located south of Whiteriver. More than a century earlier, the San Carlos Apache Reservation included the western Apache groups and others from southern Arizona and New Mexico. They had been rounded up and held in the sweltering, desertlike conditions of what became their own reservation. They hadn't had enough food or water, and their captors had been harsh. Geronimo had been a prisoner at San Carlos, and it was there that he'd rebelled against the U.S. Army and fled into the hills with a band of insurgents. On one occasion, after chasing the rebels for many miles across the dusty landscape, the cavalry came upon thirty dead horses by the side of the road. The renegades had ridden them to death and kept going on foot.

Geronimo's defiant spirit had apparently left its impression on the modern San Carlos Apache. For long-standing historical reasons, the San Carlos tribe still had resentment against the White Mountain tribe, which had cooperated with the American government and fared better during the ensuing decades. The San Carlos Apache were known for being rowdier than their counterparts to the north, as I found out when Alchesay played the San Carlos team in the mid-December tournament.

During the game, a few of their fans sat behind our bench and decided to make me the target of their abuse. It reminded me of my former life in the NBA. Some pro basketball fans, who've paid a good price for their tickets, believe this gives them the right to say anything they want to you—as if you no longer had ears or human feelings. It can get ugly and make you want to lash out at them, but that's rarely a good idea. The San Carlos fans kept calling out my name and sarcastically asking for my autograph. They threw out other insults as well. It didn't take long to figure out that they had come to the game drunk and were now wearing the nasty face of meanness that comes with being inebriated. They were loud and belligerent.

They wanted me to sign their shirts or pants. Or their body parts. They wanted me to get down on the floor and put my signature on their shoes. I tried to ignore them and watch the game, but these things are always hard to put completely out of your mind. You never know who is obnoxious and who might become dangerous. The last thing I wanted in Whiteriver was trouble, and I made a point of hustling out of the gym as soon as the game was over.

WE TOOK A LONG BREAK for the December holidays, and I went back to L.A., where a strange and wonderful thing started happening to me. People I met on the street or in restaurants treated me a little differently. They were friendlier and kinder. Those who had been following my journey to Whiteriver through the media began approaching me and congratulating me for going to the reservation and taking on this coaching job. They were intrigued by what I was doing and curious about the reservation and its people. They wanted me to tell them whatever I could about the White Mountain Apache and the kids on the team. They even talked about taking General Powell's advice and getting involved in some volunteer work of their own.

I wasn't looking for or expecting this kind of feedback, but it was gratifying to hear. My experience on the reservation was changing me in ways I was only slowly beginning to perceive. I not only felt accepted for who I was in Whiteriver, but I was also finding more acceptance by strangers in Los Angeles and other places. That was a benefit I'd never anticipated.

In early January I returned to the reservation and received a piece of good news. Something unusual had happened this year at Alchesay High over the holidays. Unlike almost every other Christmas recess in recent memory in Whiteriver, the 1998–99 basketball team did not lose a single player to partying or alcohol or drug abuse. I wanted to think that my talking to the kids about these problems had helped. I also wanted to believe that they weren't just hiding their involvement with these substances—that they really weren't using them.

We had survived the break intact and were ready to make a run for the state title.

— XVIII —

THE SEASON BEGAN IN EARNEST ON JANUARY 6, when we played Holbrook at the activity center. Our home games weren't merely sporting events, they were elaborate show-biz productions. The fanfare that now surrounded basketball at the college and pro level had filtered down to high schools and shaped the way games were presented in Whiteriver. Basketball itself was no longer enough to hold people's attention, as it had been when I'd started playing. Entertainment was the thing these days. This struck me as amusing. It was our five-time championship Los Angeles Laker teams of the 1980s that had originally been tagged with the name "Showtime," but showtime had now spread everywhere, including the White Mountain Apache reservation.

Basketball was major entertainment in Whiteriver, often the only entertainment in the wintertime. The routine before the Holbrook game was the same as it was for the others. Loud rap music greeted the fans as they poured into the gym for the girls' game and the freshmen and junior varsity boys' games. The rap, led by a rendition of the old Buffalo Springfield classic "For What It's Worth," featured a heavy beat, a stinging guitar, and a lot of slang hoop terms like "he got game," "they got game," and "we got game." It definitely loosened up the crowd and put it in more of a basketball mood. This tune was usually followed by the Village People singing "YMCA," which caused our cheerleaders to dance near the basket and our kids to rise up and shake in the stands. But the real hoopla didn't commence until the varsity team took the floor.

Before the Holbrook game, Coach Mendoza and I sat in his office, which was just off the locker room where the varsity team was dressing. He brought up some things he'd mentioned before, about the difficulties of coaching at Alchesay.

"Last year," he said, "after we lost the final game of the season by three points in the state tournament against Coolidge, our team was walking off the court. An angry parent came up to Tony and grabbed him and shook him really hard. This man blamed him for the loss. It wasn't Tony's fault. All the players made mistakes in that game, but parents can be rough. They want favors for their kids on the team, but you can't give them any favors. You've just got to get away from those people as fast as you can.

"I had a father come into the locker room and cuss at me because I took his son out late in the game. My assistant went after him and jumped on his back. I had another guy, a councilman on the tribal council, come after me because I didn't play his nephew as much as he thought I should. Others have tried to stare me down or make threats. Others have sent letters to me. You can't pay too much attention to these things."

Mendoza said all this with a smile and some laughter. He came across as a man with an amazing ability to see humor in things and keep calm. His face had a sort of glow to it, even when he was talking about people trying to intimidate him. He was trying to make it sound as if all this didn't bother him that much, but I was beginning to learn otherwise.

"Some of our players stay up very late at night," he said. "Till three or four in the morning. They're afraid of the dark. This has hurt the team because they don't get enough sleep before games. Last year during the tournament, we made them come to the gym and sleep here, but that didn't help much. They still didn't get enough rest.

"They're afraid to sleep because they have nightmares. They see things in the dark, black shadows or monsters. They hear voices in the night. Voices that tell them to do things that might be scary or dangerous."

I asked what he meant.

"Some have heard voices telling them to jump off a cliff and die. Some have heard voices telling them other ways to commit suicide. The kids talk about going down by the river next to town and seeing a man there with hooves. He's half-man, half-animal. He speaks to the kids and tells them what to do. We hear stories like this all the time. Many people around here have seen him and talked to him. They call him 'Hash.' "

I asked if he were joking with me.

"No," he said. "The kids think he's out there. That's part of the reason they can't sleep. They're thinking about him. They believe that if you go out in the dark and call for him, he'll appear."

I raised my eyebrows and Mendoza kept talking.

"I can see things and smell things that other people can't," he said. "I can see spirits following kids around. I saw three following one kid to school the other day. A boy came to me a while back. He was twelve years old. He had cancer, but he didn't know it yet. I could smell it on him, but I didn't know what to say."

"What did it smell like?"

"Not good. Like death. I didn't want to scare him or his family, but I knew he was dying. Now he's found out about the disease, and everyone knows he is dying."

Before the team took the court for tonight's game, Mendoza also mentioned to them that parents were getting angry at him because their sons weren't seeing enough playing time. He said that he had enemies on the reservation who were so upset with him over this issue that they had been using magic and witchcraft against him and some of the players. These tactics were designed to make the team fail and get him fired. He got down on the floor and drew some elaborate diagrams, illustrating what he was talking about. He said that his enemies had shaken his hand before some games and put voodoo dust on his palms, another source of bad luck.

Mendoza was a strong Christian and felt that some non-Christians among the White Mountain Apache were out to get him because of his faith. He was also convinced that one player on the team—he never said who it was—kept an owl feather under his shirt. The Apache believe that owls communicate with the dead, and the notion of that hidden feather upset the coach even more.

In the next few days, I would ask several kids if they believed that anyone was putting an evil spell on Mendoza or them. They just smiled and said no, nothing like that had happened to the team. To them, this didn't seem very real—but to Mendoza, it clearly did.

All this was strange and unsettling, serving as another reminder that I was exploring and experiencing a culture that was different from my own.

"Parents are very mad at me right now," Mendoza said to the players before the Holbrook game, "because I can't get some of you into the games. They shouldn't be mad at me, but at the starters for messing up. If the starters would do their jobs and get us ahead, then I could give everyone some minutes. Let's play up to our level and get up by forty and then everyone will see some playing time."

BUTTER BROUGHT THE GUYS TOGETHER in the locker room. They put their hands on top of one another's in a circle and all shouted: "One, two, three, Falcons!"

Then they charged out onto the court and nonchalantly moved around the basket, shooting buckets and looking stylish in their warm-ups: their shoes with no socks showing, their long shorts that reached down and touched their kneecaps, and their very short hair. More rap music played from the loudspeakers, a reprise of "For What It's Worth." The cheerleaders danced and the players swirled around them, looking confident in the way that high school kids look when people are admiring them and they've become the main attraction in a small world.

As the warm-up continued, teenage boys and girls, almost all of them dressed in black—black jackets, black sweaters, black jeans, and black socks and shoes—sat in the bleachers and gossiped. Or they clapped to the rap or worked on one another's nails or hairdos. They eyed the players and occasionally let out those high-pitched teenaged screams that cut right through your skull and echo around in your head. It must have been their hormones at work.

Hundreds and then thousands of fans streamed into the gym from every open doorway, paying three dollars a head and filling up most of the 5,000 seats, even though tonight's game would not be a sellout. Far more people attended these contests than came to those at many junior colleges.

I glanced around at the crowd. Big families with mothers, fathers, grandparents, cousins, children, grandchildren, and other relatives were sitting with one another and calling out to their kin across the way. The women were locked in talk with one another, while their husbands, many of them wearing cowboy boots and cowboy hats and blue jeans with large belt buckles, quietly took in the scene. They looked like they'd tied their paint horses to poles out in the parking lot and just stepped inside. Small kids constantly wandered out of the stands and onto the court before being dragged off by worried and scolding parents.

As Coach Mendoza sat on the bench and watched the Falcons go through their warm-up drills, a little boy came over and crawled up onto his lap. It was Anthony, his grandson, who was casually doing with him what young Cedric had done with me down in Tucson before we'd played Cholla. He was reminding him of his connections on the reservation. Mendoza patted the boy's back and smiled at him as the players continued to shoot around on the court.

This was a good moment, I told myself, a moment you wouldn't see in a lot of other places. During my pro career, I'd had people come up to me after Laker games and tell me how thankful they were because my performance that season had helped them win a $10,000 bet on the game, but that did not quite compare to what I was feeling right now. I had a sense of belonging here on the reservation, of being a part of something bigger than myself. That something wasn't just a group of people, but a family. I was finding here what I'd come for: a sense of expanding my own life and getting closer to others and building new connections following the death of my mother. I didn't have to work at doing this on the reservation; these things just came to me if I put in the time and was myself around the White Mountain Apache.

I was starting to understand the concept of family in a different and larger way. The tribe wasn't comprised merely of numerous families and clans. Everyone within the White Mountain Apache tribe was family. Everyone was connected to everyone else by blood and geography and history. That's why the Chief Alchesay Activity Center had a different atmosphere during these home games than any other gym I'd ever been in. The feeling here was warm and pervasive and enveloping. It was so much this way that it took me a while to recognize it and give it a name, because this kind of huge, sprawling, embracing family has been lost to most of modern America.

Once you've had the experience, it affects and changes you in subtle ways. It causes you to relax and open yourself up a little, to care about those around you and feel more. It makes you appreciate the value of real love, as it moves around and through a family. You can understand why it is so difficult for the young people to leave this protective environment behind and go in search of other things. Before you know it, the place has lodged itself in your heart. One evening, I stood up for the national anthem and the player introductions, and when I started to sit back down, I noticed a boy of three or four had taken my seat. His logic was clear to me: My seat was closer than most to the action on the court. I picked him up and held him aloft until his parents spotted him and waved. Then I passed him up through the stands to them.

The big family spread out in front of me in the gym this evening was truly something to witness. The old women had those ancient, wrinkled Native American faces that stir feelings deep within us. They looked like history and time itself staring back at you. Some of the old men conjured up medicine men from another age. (Last year when the Falcons had played the team representing Arizona's Hopi tribe, the Hopi had brought along not just their fans and cheerleaders, but four real medicine men dressed in traditional clothing. Throughout the game they'd prayed and performed other rituals designed to help their team win. The Alchesay side had known they were coming and, not to be outdone, had countered by bringing in four medicine men of their own to offset the effects of the Hopi. The two groups had stood at opposite ends of the floor and used their powers to influence the outcome of the game. The Hopi were victorious, but it had been close.)

The game was about to start and the music shifted again, this time to the upbeat and irresistible "Everybody Dance Now!" The crowd was already stoked, and this drove it closer to a frenzy. Our cheerleaders were leaping, and the players ran over to their respective benches. A seven-year-old boy walked out to center court and the gym fell silent. He carried a microphone and raised it to his lips, singing the national anthem in Apache, a capella, in a very high voice. He did this with fervor and a lot of feedback on the public address system, finishing to a grand ovation.

The voice of Las Vegas suddenly boomed from the big speakers attached to the ceiling. It was the recorded sound of fabled boxing announcer Michael Buffer saying, "Welcome to the main event!"

"Yes!" the fans cried from all sides of the gym. "All right!"

"Let's get ready to rumblllllle!" Buffer said, and the musical group 2 Unlimited came on with "Get Ready for This," which kept people on their feet and moving, bouncing to the rhythm.

If things had been loud earlier, they were now ear-shattering.

The players walked to the middle of the court and shook hands. A referee tossed up the opening tip-off and the game began. It was not nearly as eventful as the pregame show, and the Falcons came away with an easy victory, playing good defense and giving up only two points in the second quarter.

They ran like the wind, and made their layups and left Holbrook looking slow and flat-footed. The final score was 50–36, and the guys were very happy afterward in the locker room, congratulating one another and telling each other to go home and get some rest. They had another game two nights later, and it would be one of the best of the season.

— XIX —

THE EARLY JANUARY GAME AGAINST BLUE-
ridge, a Falcons' archrival who came from up the road at Pine-
top, was nearly as good as the three-overtime battle against
Cholla. It happened on a chilly Friday night in Whiteriver, and
by 6:30 P.M., a full hour before the varsity game started, the
parking lot outside the activity center was jammed. Teenagers
were skateboarding on the sidewalk in front of the gym or leaning on the railings and smoking cigarettes or flirting with one
another with shy smiles. Inside the lobby, things were so
crammed you could barely move through the bodies to get to
the concession stand. Security officers were roaming the halls
attempting to keep the kids from getting too rowdy. (During the
games, they tried in vain to keep them from booing our
opponents.)

When I got to the locker room, the guys were putting on
their uniforms and carrying on a deep-rooted sporting tradition:
horsing around and poking fun at one another. Tony in particular liked to tease others as he was getting dressed. Orlando Aday
liked to shadowbox with Rusty Taylor. When I asked him if he
wanted to shadowbox with me, he said, "No."

"Why?" I asked him.

"I only fight people shorter than me," he said.

He threw a make-believe punch at me and ran off laughing.

I'd been on the reservation for two months now, and the players and I had started to let down our guards with one another. They came up to me and talked now, without first asking if it was all right. They kidded me, making fun of my performance in the old comic movie *Airplane!* which they'd caught in reruns on television. They'd seen films of me playing pro basketball back in the seventies, on ESPN2, and they liked to ask what had happened to all my hair. I enjoyed the banter; it reminded me of all the other locker rooms I'd passed through in my life, where boys and men had sat together and became closer by using humor. The guys were slowly getting to know me and I was learning more about their lives off the court.

I particularly liked talking with assistant coach Tommy Parker, who always had a basketball story or a tale about his adventures on the reservation. Back in his younger days, he'd gone deer hunting with some of his friends. Tommy had long wanted to shoot a buck, and on this occasion, he spotted one in the distance in some brush. He raised his gun and fired at the creature from a ridge, hitting it squarely and sending it crumbling to the ground. He began to run toward the animal and celebrate, bragging to his buddies about what a great shot he was and how he'd finally earned his stripes as an Apache hunter. But when he and his pals reached the buck, they realized that it had been dead for some time and was propped up by the brush, making it look alive. Tommy was forever after known in Whiteriver as a hunter who could only kill dead animals.

AS I LOOKED around the locker room, studying the faces of the kids and the coaches, I had a thought, one that had been visiting me ever since I'd arrived at the reservation. I'd come here for the basketball, but that was only a piece of my experience in Whiteriver, and maybe it wasn't the most important piece. I was starting to see the kids less as ballplayers and more as human beings with entangled family lives, real challenges, and problems. They had far more to think about than hitting their layups. I wondered if basketball wasn't more of an escape for them and their fans than something to take as seriously as I always had, because my professional future lay there.

As with families everywhere, tragedy on the reservation was never far away. Throughout the season, it kept touching the team and affecting its emotions. One of our backup players, Don Ray Johnson, the kid who'd often come to practice with scars on his knuckles from fighting, had recently lost a cousin in a car wreck. Four girls had also been injured in the fatal accident. Don Ray himself had spent the Christmas season with his arm in a cast from another scuffle. He didn't swagger quite as much as he'd done back in November, but the guys still gave him plenty of space on the court. His game was growing, and he was learning to use his aggressive impulses to attack the basket whenever the defense backed off. He played relentlessly.

Loren Lupe's grandmother, who'd been instrumental in raising him, had died two weeks earlier. Since then, Loren had been even more withdrawn than usual. He was a naturally quiet young man, but the loss of this older woman had clearly affected him. He was spending more time sitting by himself in the locker room or retreating into the books he liked to read, his Shakespeare and John Grisham novels. For decades, people had been coming up to me in locker rooms and asking me why I was reading instead of talking to the other players, as if athletes should not be opening books. Now Loren was hearing the same questions. His mind hadn't been as much on basketball, but that was understandable, and all of the coaches were treating him gently and giving him time to grieve.

Over the recent Christmas holidays, Butter had gained twelve pounds. He looked like a different kid from the one I'd met back in the fall. The weight had just jumped onto his frame. He was now thicker around the chest and middle and he resembled the Michelin Man. This was not what he needed to become a quicker, better inside player, but he had apparently gone on an eating binge during the break and could not stop himself. People said he was dealing with some problems at home, but I didn't know him well enough to broach the subject.

Two days before we had played Holbrook, Sanford Tracey, a thirty-year-old relative of Rick Sanchez and Tommy Parker (and of his kids, Joe and Shasheen) had been digging a trench for a sewer at the high school. The trench had instantly collapsed, killing Tracey. The death had rocked everyone at Alchesay High, causing the school to shut down for the rest of the day, but the loss was especially devastating for Rick, who disappeared from practice for a while afterward.

Then a twelve-year-old boy who had followed the Falcons closely and had once been allowed to ride the team bus died of cancer. This was the same boy whom Coach Mendoza had said he could smell death on a few weeks earlier. His death shocked the squad and stunned the whole community. They all learned once again, as they had many times before in Whiteriver, that there is nothing sadder than burying a young person in the cemetery at the edge of town.

Coach Mendoza himself was proving to be a complicated and

provocative man. He had become increasingly obsessed in the locker room with tales of witchcraft and how magic was being used against him or the players on the team. He spent valuable practice time talking about how he was there to help the guys if any of them had problems with the supernatural forces that were aligned against them.

The boys were a captive audience and could do nothing but listen to him speak about evil manipulations and sorcerers. I listened too, but believed that a high school basketball coach really didn't have the right to talk constantly to the players about things that only he seemed to be aware of. Parents and religious counselors were better prepared to deal with these areas. I felt strongly about this, but I was just an assistant coach in these circumstances and kept my silence. Every player I spoke to regarding these issues told me that he did not really understand what Mendoza was talking about.

WITHIN AND AROUND all of these events, our players were steadily working on their games at practice and trying to improve. In the recent tournament at Alchesay High— and before he had gained the twelve pounds—Butter had asserted himself and been named the Most Valuable Player. He had the ability to be a team leader and was big enough at six feet, two inches to be both a good inside and outside threat, but the weight needed to come off. He wasn't a good jumper to begin with, and the extra pounds did not help either his leaping or his confidence. In basketball terminology, he "played small."

On the other hand, Willie Zagotah, who was about the same height, played big. He was continuing to improve and impress. Willie had discovered that he really could jump and bump under the basket. He'd figured out that despite having lean muscles, he was stronger than he'd imagined and was definitely stretching his game. I'd been working daily on getting him to time his efforts to block opponents' shots, and I loved watching him leap through the air and swat away the ball. He was giving us some good, tough minutes off the bench and had a chance to become a starter. He was also moving, on and off the court, with far more spring in his step than when the season had started.

Ivan was also coming along. I was getting to know not only him, but also his stepfather, Bill Walker, who sometimes dropped in on practice, and his mother, Deborah, who worked at the local grocery store. Walker had lately approached me at practice and told me that I needed to know some things about the big kid from Louisiana. According to his stepdad, Ivan had had a rough childhood. His biological father had been a very uptight, controlling parent who had been hypercritical of almost everything the boy had done. Ivan had always felt that he could do little that was right in his father's eyes. So today, Walker explained to me, the teenager had a lot of trouble distinguishing between useful criticism and being ripped for no good purpose or being told that he was a failure. He didn't really understand that there was such a thing as constructive criticism, or that when adults pointed out what he needed to work on, they were trying to help him, not hurt him. He was basically, from what I was being told, still traumatized from his early experiences.

For all these reasons, Ivan tended to freeze up on the court when he made a mistake—or to get lost in the moment when he did something right—rather than staying in the flow of the game.

I told Walker (who had served in the modern Tenth Cavalry

of the U.S. Army and was very knowledgeable about its history and the Buffalo Soldiers) that I greatly appreciated receiving this information about his stepson and would try to filter it into my coaching sessions with him. It made me want Ivan to succeed even more. He was definitely playing better, more consistent basketball, and with improvement, he too had a shot at becoming a starter before the season ended.

The other kids liked Ivan and had clearly accepted him onto the team. One afternoon at practice, when the players were missing a lot of layups, Don Ray Johnson jokingly blamed it on Ivan. He said something that echoed the history of the tribe and its interaction with outsiders.

"He's the white man," Don Ray said, pointing at Ivan, "who brought the disease to the reservation."

The disease, in this case, was their inability to make their shots.

Everyone, including Ivan, laughed at the remark and continued the drill.

SINCE TONY AND I had had our confrontation at practice, he hadn't been talking as much and had shown that he could take coaching instructions. He was playing somewhat more under control and with some respect for the mental aspects of the game. He had talent, but until now he hadn't realized how much of the game is played with your head. He still chafed at slowing down the game and running set plays—he liked to fly up and down the court with the ball in his hands—but he was trying to make some changes. I cautiously regarded this as a small but sweet victory.

Kyle was having a great year. He was as good as people had

said he was. He was not only our best scorer, but he did the tough things like rebounding, playing defense, and hitting the floor for loose balls, which you have to do to have a complete game.

He had the instincts of a real player, which is something you can't teach. Pro or college scouts who attend games looking for talent are always searching for players who can "create off the dribble." That means they can make something happen by themselves by passing to an open man, getting off their own shot when covered or even double-covered, getting fouled and making free throws, or doing something else to help the team. They aren't dependent on set plays or their teammates but can find their own scoring opportunities. Kyle was like that; he could make things happen. He had an innate sense of how to take the ball to the basket and not be stopped, regardless of who was in front of him.

Scouts also look for players who aren't afraid to put up shots when the game is "on the line." Many guys don't want the ball in the last few seconds of a close game, because they're fearful of making a mistake or missing a basket that costs their team a victory. When the season started, I had hopes for the Falcons' Jon Leonard, but after sustaining a couple of minor injuries and committing a few small errors in a game, he didn't want to take any more risks and soon found himself on the bench. The best players know that you can't win without taking chances and aren't much bothered by the prospect of failure. If they missed their last shot, they believe that the next one will go in. (Think of Larry Bird putting up all those late-in-the-game shots under pressure.) Kyle was never afraid to step forward when someone had to.

And yet, Kyle's dominant skills on the court also had a drawback. I was starting to wonder if maybe he weren't too good for us to have a balanced attack.

Tinker, Joe Parker, Orlando, and Blaine Goklish were giving us a lot of effort, but as the season moved along, you could see that it was Kyle's team—just as last year it had been Armando Cromwell's—and this represented another conflict that ran below the surface of the Falcons squad.

To keep winning, we needed more involvement from everyone, but when we got behind in games, the other guys, even Brennen and Tony, tended to stand around and let Kyle take over. He was a natural at doing this and not shy about assuming control. In a sense, you wanted him to run the show because he excelled at it, but in another sense, you didn't want him to do that. One terrific player usually cannot beat the other team, but you didn't dare curb his instincts for the game. This was a quandary, and none of the coaches knew what to do about it.

AS I LOOKED at the kids in the locker room before they took the floor for the Blueridge contest, I wished there were more minutes in the games so that Don Ray, Tinker, Orlando, Blaine, and Joe, among others, could get more playing time. They needed it and deserved it for working hard in practice, but the minutes just weren't available for everyone to have an equal chance.

I also wished there were more weeks in our season, which was quickly slipping by. Whenever I thought about how fast time was moving, I had a sense of vertigo. It seemed that I'd just gotten here, yet my days on the reservation were more than half used up. I wanted to slow things down and savor them, but that wasn't possible, because there was always work to do.

The longer I coached the kids, the more I realized that there simply weren't enough weeks left to convey many of the things I'd wanted to. Time was already running out and all I could do was offer some new concepts and hope that they practiced them on their own after I was gone.

— XX —

WE BEGAN THE BLUERIDGE GAME PLAYING WELL. The Falcons were learning to do the things we'd been drilling into them day after day. They weren't making as many bad passes or flying up and down the court and flinging up wild shots. They weren't jumping up in the air with no idea of what to do next, but keeping their feet on the floor until they were ready to make a move. They were actually running two set plays, working the ball in closer to the basket, taking better shots, and making more of them. This might have seemed like a small thing to someone not familiar with Alchesay basketball, but it was a great stride compared to what I'd seen that first day at practice. I had influenced their style of play.

Tinker Burnette was hitting some open shots this evening, and Kyle was hot. We quickly went up 16–8 and it looked as if this would be an easy win. Floyd Massey, the legendary public address announcer for the Falcons, was having a good time tonight with the large crowd. He took his cue from some microphone showmen in the NBA, particularly the announcers for the Chicago Bulls and the old Philadelphia 76ers. Whenever one of our guys scored, Floyd boomed out: "Two for Butter!"

"Tinker for three!"

"That's our Tony Parker!"

"Kyle again!"

Or simply: "Blaine!"

"Ivannnnn Lamkinnnnn!"

When Willie went way up in the air for a rebound, Floyd said, "Let's hear it for Sky Zagotah!"

Massey liked to provide running commentary not just on the action on the court but on public events inside of and beyond the city limits of Whiteriver. During a time-out early in the Blueridge game, he referred to President Clinton's troubles in office by saying, "If you want to know what's going on with the impeachment trial, call the folks over at FATCO!"

Then he embarrassed a visiting *Los Angeles Times* reporter by giving her a huge White Mountain Apache welcome, introducing her to the screaming fans and telling her to stand up. She declined.

When one of the officials made a call that went against the Falcons, Massey said, "The ref's contact fell out on that play. Could somebody help him find it?"

The second quarter was the exact opposite of the first. We faltered by making bad passes and let Blueridge back in the game. Blueridge had obviously scouted us and were playing smart. They used a zone defense instead of man-to-man. In man-to-man, one player on defense matches up against one player on offense; this usually allows for offensive players to be more creative. Our guards, Kyle and Tony and Tinker, because of their quickness and agility, were at their best against man-to-man defenses.

In a zone defense, each of the five opposition players covers a spot on the floor instead of a single man. Zones tend to slow everything down and cause offenses to rely either on their long-range shooting or working the ball inside. Neither of these was our strong point, and the Blueridge zone took away some of our spontaneity and speed. We not only started making errant passes but were standing around on the court, waiting for something to happen instead of creating. We wanted the guys to run their set plays, but the downside of that strategy was that sometimes the kids slowed down so much they almost became spectators.

Throughout the second quarter, Blueridge came scrapping back and we led by only 28–27 at the half. Near the end of the half, Ivan entered the game and gave us some good minutes, blocking shots and grabbing rebounds. I'd been working with him on both of these areas, and there was a glimmer of focus, determination, and confidence that hadn't been there before.

In the locker room during the break, I told the kids to tighten up on defense and think before passing the ball. We could win the game by using our heads, but lose it through mental laziness. We were better than Blueridge, I said, but only if we played them as smart as they were playing us.

Butter gathered the guys around him and they all reached out their hands and gave the yell: "One, two, three, Falcons!" Then he led them out onto the court for the second half.

In the third quarter, we continued to stumble, unable to find the rhythm that had carried us through the first part of the game. Basketball is a sport that flows when you're playing well. When the flow stops, you're never quite sure why this has happened, just as you're never exactly sure why the shots you were making earlier suddenly won't go in. At the center of the game is a mysterious movement of energy, back and forth and back and forth again, that can never be tamed or fully understood.

I sat on the bench next to Tommy Parker, growing discouraged. We'd all but stopped running our plays and looking for good shots. In the face of adversity, we had forgotten the things we'd worked on in practice. The crowd was getting discouraged, too. I could hear some remarks coming out of the stands and a few boos. They'd come here to see action—the kind of full-court, all-out basketball they were used to seeing their team play—and what they were getting was flat and stale.

Tony, in particular, was making bad passes and turnovers. I looked over at Coach Mendoza, wanting him to take the guard out and sit him down, but Mendoza wouldn't do that. I wanted him to show Tony that there was a price to be paid for playing out of control, but Mendoza had difficulty benching one of his starters. All players have bad games and need to be benched, even in the pros. Coaches have to do this in order to establish themselves as the team leaders and authority figures. They have to make the hard decisions for the good of everyone, but Mendoza did not want to hurt anyone's feelings.

As a coach, you only get really upset with the kids who have talent, and Tony did. He had enough athletic gifts, if he used them, to go on to a small college and get a scholarship to play ball, so he could continue his education both on the court and in the classroom. He had the goods but not the discipline—at least not yet.

At one point during a time-out, I almost started to speak to Mendoza and say that the moment had come to get Tony's attention—in the middle of a close game—and let him know that if he kept playing like a hot dog and hurting the team, he was going to ride the bench.

It was an awkward situation, so I didn't say anything. I sat back down on the bench and watched, becoming more frustrated. There was something between Tony and me, something that had been there from the start, and it hadn't completely worked itself out. He was a cocky kid, and I respected his brass—even admired it in some ways. Most good athletes have some of that, but I still wanted to let him know that the coaches, not the players, ran the team.

From the end of the first quarter to the end of the third quarter, Blueridge outscored us 32–16. We went into the fourth period trailing 43–34, and the game looked out of reach. With only four minutes to go, we were still behind 49–40, and while some of the fans were now booing louder, many older people had risen from their seats and were heading for the exits. A lot of grandmothers and grandfathers wanted to get out to the parking lot first and get a jump on the other drivers heading home. There was disgruntled murmuring in the crowd and disappointment in the fans leaving the building. Even the war cries had gone silent.

Kyle hit a shot. He stole the ball and hit another, bringing us to within five points with 80 seconds left. He got the ball again and scored.

"That's Kyle!" Floyd Massey said.

Fans who had been heading for the exits were returning to their seats, and fans who had stayed put would not sit down, giving Kyle a standing ovation. A gym that had been dead a few minutes earlier was surging with movement and noise.

It was as if Kyle had been holding back and waiting for this moment to arrive—when the team had no choice but to stand aside and let him do everything.

The better he played, the louder the fans roared. The faster he ran, the more teenage shrieks filled the gym. War cries started to roll out of the stands from every direction and crawl up my neck again.

I wanted the team to win by doing things the right way, because that was how I'd been taught to play the game. The Falcons and their fans just wanted a hero to lead them to victory. I leaned back and watched Kyle take charge.

He brought the ball up the court and drove toward the basket, wending his way through several taller opponents and taking it all the way in for a layup that bounced off the glass and fell through the net.

"Kyle, one more time!" Floyd cried.

We were down only 50–47.

As the Falcons retreated back on defense, Massey shouted above the din: "Folks, it's nail-eating time!"

Blueridge threw the ball away and eight thousand feet began to stomp on the metal stands. The gym was trembling and the teenage yelling kicked up another notch. I'd forgotten all about Tony and his miscues. Like everyone else in the building, I was out of my seat and my eyes were fixed on Kyle. The same thing I'd seen against Cholla was surfacing again: When all appeared lost, Apache basketball came rushing out and swept across the team and its fans. Our best warrior emerged and was fearless with the ball.

Kyle drove the length of the floor again and took off at the free throw line, soaring toward the goal. He released the ball in a soft arc and it fell through the rim.

The score was 50–49, with 38 seconds to go.

"Kyle—yes!" Massey said through the pandemonium.

Blueridge inbounded the ball and Kyle fouled one of their players, who hit both free throws, making it 52–49.

Kyle drove the ball upcourt, but this time instead of shooting he passed it off to Tony, who put up a three-point shot that sailed in.

I was yelling as loudly as everyone else, and for the moment I had forgotten or forgiven Tony for all his previous sins.

The game was tied at 52 and Blueridge had the ball.

A time-out was called and the public address system now played the most famous of all sporting event songs: Gary Glitter's "Rock 'n' Roll, Part One," during which the band plays and yells, "Hey!" and everyone in the stands is supposed to yell "Hey!" in unison with them. Everyone in the gym did just that, while people danced in the aisles, shouting out "Kyle!" and "Tony!" It was a total celebration of the game and, win or lose, the best thing going on in Whiteriver on a Friday night, a modern ritual that let people know they could win.

Blueridge came down, shot, and missed. Ivan rebounded with only seconds remaining. He got the ball to Kyle, who ran the ball up the court, twisting and bending through traffic, and took another shot. This one bounced away, but he'd been fouled and would shoot free throws with less than three ticks on the clock. As the war cries ceased and everyone became quiet, Kyle stood on the line and took a couple of dribbles before aiming his shot.

The first one went in. So did the next one. We were ahead 54–52, but Blueridge would have one last try. They called a time-out and the teams went over to their benches. Our guys were drenched and bent over from exertion. They knew what to do next—play good defense but don't foul—so nobody said much of anything.

"Are you enjoying the game now?" Massey asked the crowd.

It groaned. This game was too close to enjoy.

Blueridge threw the ball in. One of their players drove hard and tossed up a 25-foot shot that arced toward the rim, looking on target, while everyone in the gym followed its flight as it descended to the goal.

It clanked off the iron and fell away, hitting the floor and ending the game.

The Falcons ran across the court and off the bench and tackled one another toppling over together in a pile of arms and legs and wet yellow jerseys. Fans left the stands and came out to hug them. Little kids who had been playing under the bleachers instead of watching the game now emerged and joined in the fun.

On the other side of the floor, the Blueridge players stared at the happy chaos and were motionless, stunned by the loss.

The PA system struck up "YMCA" and our guys untangled from the pile and lined up for the ceremonial handshake with the other team that followed all of our games. Then the Falcons dashed into the locker room while the coaches moved closely behind them, all of us beaming from the victory. Winning feels good not because the other team has been defeated, but because your kids' hard work has paid off and produced a tangible result. In this case, there was cheering, back-slapping, and huge smiles all around.

Inside the locker room, as they stood there sweating and shaking hands and giving high-fives, too pumped up to sit down, I said to them, "We turned the ball over too many times, guys. If we hadn't done that, we would have won easily. The ball is precious. You've still got to learn that. We have to treat the ball that way and protect it better. But this was a great win. You attacked when you got behind and you never quit."

Then Coach Mendoza said, "Defense turned it around for us, but we got sloppy after the first half. We can't play like a bunch of Indians for three quarters and then play like Apache in the last three minutes."

Everybody laughed and cheered some more.

Brennen brought them together for one more loud, "One, two, three, Falcons!" and they headed for the showers.

I ducked out and started to leave the gym, but when I got back to the court, I noticed that many people were still lingering there, not ready to go home yet, relishing the afterglow of the triumph. Women were carrying babies and stopping to talk, exchanging "Happy New Years" with each other. Men were grinning and looking younger and very proud. Kids were running up and down the floor, reenacting what had just taken place in the game and imitating Tony and Kyle. The music was still playing—an old Creedence Clearwater classic "Susie Q"—and teenagers were dancing with one another or by themselves.

Over the PA, Floyd Massey mentioned the purses and items of clothing that had been lost or left behind, asking fans to come and pick them up before departing. The game and the win were still alive in the gym; people could feel that and wanted to hold on to it for a while longer.

I stepped outside and saw Tony already out there, the first player to leave our locker room. His hair was wet, but he wore a big smile and was surrounded by kids who were telling him that he'd done a great job tonight. He looked like a young hero and was drinking in the glory.

As I pulled out of the parking lot, I saw an old man walking alone through the chilly darkness. He wore blue jeans and a cowboy hat and was limping along the side of the road. He was just visible in the headlights of the cars as they moved past him. Somehow I knew that it had been worth it for him, and for all of us, to come out tonight and watch the Falcons play.

I turned north, heading out of Whiteriver. A long stream of taillights was in front of me—all the other cars going home. I flipped on the radio, 88.1 FM, and heard the man behind the microphone say in a combination of English and Apache that Alchesay had just won their game against Blueridge 54–52, and it had been a great one. He gave out a howl of delight and cued up another rock classic, which perfectly fit the mood of the evening: George Thorogood's "Bad to the Bone."

It was a fine salute to the Falcons.

— XXI —

FIVE MILES SOUTHEAST OF WHITERIVER IS THE Fort Apache Cultural Center. On warm and sunny winter days, before practice started, I liked to drive out there and look at the old homes and brick buildings that had once made up the fort. I liked to sit quietly and listen to the crows cawing as they circled overhead near the mesas, and hear the wind as it blew through the towering pines. Walking around the grounds, I felt the past beneath my feet, and I would visit the round-shaped cultural center itself, where there were books and photographs on Apache history and displays showing how Apache women had woven the baskets that were once central to their way of life.

It was right here, more than three years earlier, that I'd met Edgar Perry, and our meeting had eventually brought me to the reservation to coach. I had come in search of a Buffalo Soldier named John Glass, the chief of scouts at Fort Apache, whose picture I had seen in several publications and whose face and story had haunted me from the moment I'd come across them. I hadn't been able to find much about him at the fort, where he had served in the U.S. Cavalry, but I was driven to learn more about Glass's life.

I contacted Paul Bucher, an East Coast archivist, who located Glass's military pension records within the U.S. government.

Glass was born in Polk County, Georgia, and had enlisted in the Tenth Cavalry in Atlanta in December 1876. He'd had a wife, son, and daughter, and he had applied for disability compensation in 1902 because of damaged hearing. He was deaf in both ears by the time he died in 1908. On February 20, 1891, he had shot and killed a Sergeant George Foster. The cause of the dispute was mentioned nowhere. Glass was put in the guardhouse to await action by the authorities, but what happened after that remains unknown.

At first, the information about Sgt. Foster's death startled me, and it took me a while to face it squarely. I had always viewed the Buffalo Soldiers in heroic terms, but now I realized that not all of the events in their history in the Southwest had involved heroism. I had wanted to uncover only those things in Glass's past that had been flattering and complimentary, but that view diminishes the harsh frontier violence of the times that he had served in while in the military. Only confronting the fuller truth of his life and actions genuinely honors his memory.

MANY THINGS about Glass reminded me of later American military history and conjured up memories of my dad. Glass had played the trumpet in the army band. (My father was a trombonist.) My dad had received artillery training in the army during World War II, but the military hierarchy had been determined to keep segregation intact and not let African Americans fight alongside whites. This attitude had been set in place prior to World War I, when a black colonel, Charles Young, was in line to become a general and have white soldiers take orders from him. He was soon declared "medically unfit for service" and never assumed command. In such ways, black soldiers were kept in their subservient military roles as manual laborers, steve-dores, and truck drivers.

During World War II, the army establishment had still not dared to offend Southerners, so men like my father had never gotten the chance to defend their country on the battlefield. Fifty years later, in the 1990s, he was still bitter about this. (The best thing that came out of his service was that while on leave one weekend, he met my mother.) He'd spent his time in the military playing trombone in the army band. I've often wondered if my lifelong attraction to military history and artifacts—to the nineteenth-century guns, swords, maps, and buckskin uniforms on the walls of my L.A. home—is because my father never got to fight as a soldier.

Some black men had more opportunities and did see combat in World War II. My dad and I have always regarded them as heroes. One soldier we both knew well was a retired New York City police officer named Leonard "Smitty" Smith.

Shortly before Thanksgiving in 1998, I briefly left the reserva-tion to return to Los Angeles and bring together my dad and Smitty for a long-awaited reunion. For many years, Smitty had closely followed my basketball career, and after my retirement our paths crossed again because I'd been asked to work on a documentary about the liberation of Nazi death camps by black troopers in World War II.

The film, based on the book *Liberators: Fighting on Two Fronts in World War II*, featured one African-American unit in particular, the 761st Battalion. Despite racism in the army and Jim Crow segregation, the 761st had performed extremely well in the Battle of the Bulge and the liberation of several genocidal camps. It was only after I saw Smitty at the film's premiere that

I became aware he had been a member of the 761st though I had known him since I was eleven or twelve years old.

I took a few days off from my coaching duties in Whiteriver to be with my dad and Smitty, so they could reminisce about being policemen in New York.

Maybe I was fulfilling both my father's dream and my own by coming to the reservation and following in John Glass's footsteps, working with the White Mountain Apache people. Maybe I wasn't looking for Glass's history as much as I was looking for myself—or at least looking to carry on his work more than a century earlier. I had come to the tribe in 1998 to make new friends and work together with the White Mountain Apache for a common purpose.

In the 1870s, Native Americans and African Americans had joined together to bring peace to the region, to cooperate with one another in settling the West. I had come to the reservation to share my knowledge of basketball and cooperate with the local people as we strived toward a common goal. The conditions for all of us had changed dramatically, but we were still trying to break down the walls that separated us as human beings.

The fate of the team—the win-loss record of the Falcons—didn't seem so important to me as I walked around Fort Apache in the warm winter sunshine and took in the past. It was the interaction with the tribe that counted, the daily contact with others who were like myself—but unlike myself—in so many different ways.

FORT APACHE had a cemetery for its scouts and other military personnel. I liked to explore it, but on other occasions when I wanted to experience the White Mountain

Apache past, I walked to the large cemetery in Whiteriver, which lay on a hillside just a few blocks from the gymnasium. Tall nonflowering cacti stood over the graves, many of them surrounded by small white picket fences or covered with vases of colorful plastic flowers or small American flags. Some held statues of Jesus or the Virgin Mary. Some had crosses made of wood or carved stone. Others had signs that said things like "World's Greatest Grandma." The most elaborate gravestones were often for babies that had been born and died on the same day.

The cemetery was slightly above the rest of the town, so the sunlight here was particularly intense and a breeze swept up red dust from graves and scattered it over the tombstones. You could look out over the whole valley that held Whiteriver and see blue smoke climbing from the stacks at FATCO. The deep silence of the small village going about its daily business was pervasive and calming.

As you stood among the dead, two things were most striking. First, many of the headstones told of the military service that the deceased had given to the United States. The White Mountain Apache had been proud of fighting for their country against renegade Indians back in the nineteenth century, and they were just as proud of having fought for America in its twentieth-century wars. Second, a lot of the graves had Hispanic names written on them. These weren't the actual names of the dead, but names that had been given to them. Some had taken Spanish surnames because their real names were secrets, known only inside their clans.

Graveyards are mysterious places, especially on Indian reservations, where the names have been changed on markers and many people have died young, where the past is slowly fading away like the deteriorating numbers and letters on the stone and wooden crosses that designate the dead. So many lives were spread out on the ground before me. Graveyards have a special feeling when the wind kicks up and blows dust across your face, then settles back onto the ancient earth before swirling up again.

I never stayed in this one very long.

— XXII —

OUR NEXT GAME WAS AGAINST ROUND VALLEY, and it turned out to be another classic. The more I coached the Falcons, the more I realized that basketball excitement was pretty much the same at every level of the sport—only the number of fans watching, the amount of money at stake, and the talent of the players were different. People could get just as crazed in a jam-packed high school gym watching a group of teenagers battle it out on the court as they could watching a group of highly paid pro athletes go against each other at the Boston Garden or the Forum in L.A. We come to the games looking for displays of passion and the will to win, and those things can spring up anywhere.

Although I'd initially come to Whiteriver with the idea of eventually coaching in the NBA, my mind was starting to change. More than anything else, I liked teaching and having the time to work with players one-on-one in practice. I liked to study how they played—to break down their style and improve the little things, the subtle things, that can help a player develop. Things like positioning oneself under the basket for a rebound, using the body to keep a defender at arm's length, and employing both hands to score near the goal. I liked the aesthetics of basketball and helping a player become not just more efficient but more fluid and graceful on the court. I was big on the details.

Pro players were inherently more difficult to teach than others because they were older and had already had great success doing things their way. They were also making more money than their coaches, and their schedule was so grueling that there wasn't much time left over for practicing or learning new things. It was a rare individual who really wanted to stretch his game after he'd become a professional.

High school coaching represented a lot of challenges, too. The kids were going through so many emotional and physical things besides playing basketball that it was hard for them to focus on just the game. Most of them did not have an abundance of talent or size or a great feel for the sport. Among the Falcons, there were only five kids who really looked and moved like basketball players, with their sleek, quick, well-muscled bodies. They were the brothers Kyle and Blaine Goklish, Willie Zagotah, Loren Lupe, and Tony Parker. Willie alone on the front line could play the vertical game—he could jump with real spring in his legs. Most of the other guys resisted going inside because they knew they couldn't get off the floor, but Willie was different. If I'd had another month or two to work with him, I would have had him dunking the ball while his opponents were staring up at him, and that would have rattled the walls of the Chief Alchesay Activity Center during home games. From what I'd seen so far, there was no dunking on the reservation.

From childhood, I had been drawn to academic subjects such as history, and if I hadn't been over seven feet tall and good at basketball, I might have ended up a professor. I was starting to think that instead of the pros or high school, a college coaching position might be the right balance point for me. You could still reach and teach guys in their early twenties, but you weren't confronting all the hormones, vulnerabilities, and psychological crises of teenage boys. The idea of working in a university setting, around people with some of the same interests as mine, held a lot of appeal for me.

For decades, I'd made my living in the sports realm, where reading and thinking were considered eccentric, and where many sportswriters were more comfortable with athletes who didn't shatter the stereotype of the dumb jock. I'd never conformed to that stereotype and that had hung over my head from the moment I entered the public arena. I didn't act the way others thought I was supposed to act and didn't give people respect simply because they felt they deserved it from me. I performed when on the court, but the rest of my life was my own. I didn't smile when, or as much as, others thought I should or as much as some other famous athletes did. That wasn't my personality and I couldn't change this or explain it to most people. I smiled when something was funny or when I felt like smiling.

In November 1998, an article appeared in *Sports Illustrated* with quotes from my former teammates—Kurt Rambis in particular—about their views of me from my playing days. Magic Johnson had also taken a shot at me about marijuana use on *The Magic Hour*. I have been heavily criticized for using marijuana although I have a medical prescription from the state of California to use marijuana legally for migraine headaches. I had shown support for Magic when he'd tested positive for HIV and I expected more from a former teammate. I had worked as hard as I could to be reliable on the court, to help the team win, and to insure success for the Lakers. I had stayed in shape and wanted those championship rings as much as anyone else. I thought that was enough and that all of us had gotten along well, but time has illuminated the reality behind the facade of camaraderie. The *Sports Illustrated* article and Magic's actions put everything into a different perspective for me.

My attitude or way of being has long offended some people, but that has only made me want to be more myself. Being African American has compounded the difficulty. There were always those who had trouble realizing that—despite my appearance— my inner world could be as rich, complex, unique, and unlimited as anyone else's. Maybe at heart, I'd always wanted to be a scholar as well as an athlete, and maybe I would be more at peace in the academic world.

Or maybe the right opportunity in the NBA simply hadn't come along yet. One thing was for certain: The kids had rekindled my passion for basketball. After leaving Whiteriver, I wanted to stay connected to the sport and keep coaching. I was back in the game, and that's exactly where I wanted to be.

Another thing was also certain: The longer I was away from L.A., the more I understood that I wasn't just taking a casual break from my old life. I was building new relationships after losing some irreplaceable ones from my past; I was closing some circles. I was searching for another home.

— XXIII —

"WE'RE COMING TOGETHER AS A TEAM," RUSTY Taylor said in the locker room before the Round Valley game. He was always good for a dose of enthusiasm and optimism. "We're getting better, and that's supposed to happen at this time of the season. It makes me hopeful for what we can do later on. We had more talent last year, but that team didn't play as much with their heads. This one is trying to do that, to work on the mental part of the game and do what the coaches tell them. I look at kids' faces to see desire. You have to be able to see desire in their eyes to know how far they can go when they reach the regional and state tournaments. I know that they're improving, but I don't know how much desire is there."

I wanted to agree with Rusty, but wasn't entirely convinced by his words. I thought the kids' desire was there—ever since early December, they had been practicing with more intensity—but I was still worried about the fundamentals. They were trying to change their game, and it was not a smooth process; sitting on the bench, I could almost hear the gears grinding out on the court.

During warm-ups, the PA system played Barry White as the kids shot layups and jumpers and passed the ball around. As White's basso profundo voice filled the gym, I looked around for

Edgar Perry, who always came to the games with a grandniece or other young relative. He was sitting behind me, holding a little girl on his lap. I walked over to him and we talked for a while about Shasheen, Edgar's niece. She had been studying to prepare herself for college to become a doctor. Her grades, especially in math, were getting better, and we were both very proud of her. Some day I hope to go back to the reservation and write a book about the Apache medical clinic she is running in Whiteriver.

I'd recently interviewed the seniors on the Falcons' cheerleading squad about their ambitions. I'd wanted to know more about some of the young women at Alchesay High. Four of the cheerleaders would graduate this year and all of them intended to go on to college with the scholarship money available to them. Alison Numkeena wanted to become a social worker and return to Whiteriver to help the local kids. Jovana Aday was interested in studying child psychology, while Patricia Lee, the only white girl on the squad, was determined to become an architect. Natasha Bryce planned to go to law school and also use her training to assist the tribe.

Speaking with the four of them had only deepened my sense that Apache teenage girls were more focused and grounded than many of the young men at the high school. They had a clear sense of purpose and responsibility, seemed older than their years, and held an accurate vision of themselves and their futures.

OUR STARTERS against Round Valley were pretty much the same as when the season had begun: Tony and Kyle at guards, Butter at center, Loren and Blaine at forwards.

Ivan and Willie were getting more playing time, but hadn't quite cracked the opening lineup. I was still waiting and hoping for that day to arrive.

Round Valley, like so many of the other teams, was taller than the Falcons. They were scrappy and the game would be hard fought from beginning to end. The score was tied at eleven and then thirteen, with the Falcons taking a 17–15 lead at the close of first quarter. Ivan entered the game and began exerting himself, playing big and continuing the good work he'd been giving us in recent weeks. He hit a basket to make it 22–19, and then another to further increase our lead. He grabbed some rebounds and moved the Round Valley kids out from under the basket with his hips and shoulders. He blocked a shot. He was gaining more and more confidence, not standing around on the floor nearly as much as he had a few months earlier. Ivan was getting to know his body and what it could do when he pushed it. He was much stronger than he realized. If I'd only gotten to him sooner. . . .

Halfway through the second quarter, to the dismay of the big crowd, the PA announcer informed everyone in the gym that the concession stand had run dry.

"The food is sold out!" Floyd Massey said. "No pop or popcorn!"

The fans groaned.

"No candy!" Floyd said.

People roared their disapproval.

"Nothing! Zilch!"

A small girl with a white feather in her pure black hair wandered by the bench, as if looking for her parents. I kept my eye on her for a few moments, wondering if she were lost, then turned back to the game.

One of the refs made a bad call against Ivan, and the crowd let the official hear it. A few minutes later, the other ref made an even worse call against Ivan, and the people in the stands increased their catcalling and heckling. Folks on the reservation were starting to like this big kid and feel he was one of theirs. Like me, he was becoming part of the family.

Ivan and Willie were banging under the boards. Several other Falcons were also playing more physical basketball than when the season had started. We'd made some progress together since I'd asked Loren to put his hand on the waist of a teammate during an early practice and he'd looked at me as if I'd gone mad. The kids would bump and handcheck now, but they were still restrained compared to the way the game was played in many other places.

The White Mountain Apache, I'd come to see, were modest people when it came to using and displaying their bodies. They didn't do a lot of touching in public or show other, more aggressive kinds of affection. The kids didn't flirt much with one another, and girls didn't wear low-cut blouses or revealing skirts. Their grace and sensuality were present in all that they did, but they'd been taught not to flaunt these things in front of other people or their family members.

THE GAME was heating up. Ivan was having one of his best games ever, At the half, the score was tied 26–26.

In the locker room during the break, I praised the kids for being so aggressive and told them to keep Round Valley from getting "in the paint"—basketball parlance for moving in close to the goal and taking a high-percentage shot.

"Seal off the middle of the court," I said. "Keep their players out of the lane and away from the basket. Don't let them penetrate, and if they try to, get in front of them and stand your ground. We've got to keep the pressure on them now."

In the second half, the game intensified, but we were starting to falter. Tony was again having a tough night. As had happened before, he put up bad shots and made some errant passes. We fell behind 36–29, and once more I wanted Coach Mendoza to sit Tony down and let him cool off and think about his play. But that didn't happen. By this point in the season, I'd more or less resigned myself to this pattern. Some things were so deeply ingrained that to tamper with them would start more trouble than it would have been worth.

What had happened many times this season now happened again. The further down we got, the more ferociously we began to play. With a minute to go in the third quarter, our defenders inadvertently sent one of their players to the floor, busting open his chin. For several seconds, the crowd was silent and fearful, afraid he'd been knocked unconscious, and when the kid finally stirred and stood up, he received a huge ovation.

As all this was unfolding, I looked around and noticed the little girl with the white feather in her hair. She was no longer wandering near the court with a lost expression in her eyes, but was up in the stands lying in her mother's arms, crying. It was after nine o'clock, and the excitement must have been too much for her.

In the fourth quarter, Round Valley played extremely well and we fell further behind. The things I had been telling the kids all season were coming true on the floor tonight. Pure effort was not enough. Scrambling wildly on the floor was not enough. Giving everything you had was good, but it was better if you played under control throughout the game, worked the ball inside, and didn't rely so much on Kyle and Tony.

The team's essential weakness was too obvious tonight to ignore. We needed more players to be involved, especially needed our big guys to contribute more during all four quarters instead of just in spurts. We needed more of Ivan and Willie, but this was crunch time and that meant one thing for the Falcons. They would revert to the only game they knew how to play and turn everything over to their star.

With five minutes to go, Round Valley went up by a dozen and the action got nastier. Tony sent another of their players to the floor, but he jumped up quickly and wasn't really hurt. Round Valley's coach was upset by the roughness and began complaining to the officials. The crowd disliked this and unleashed their disapproval. Everyone was up and yelling. The gym had filled with tension, and chaos was in the air. If one more player went down, things could turn ugly.

War cries were flying across the gym, and people were on their feet, pounding the metal stands. Even Floyd Massey felt things had gone far enough.

"We want everyone to calm down," the PA announcer said, and for once he wasn't making a joke. "If you can't control yourselves, the security force here will help you leave."

Time-out was called. People sat down and the noise level in the stands eventually fell. Music came on—"YMCA"—and the cheerleaders began to smile and dance. The tension subsided, and Floyd had helped accomplish that.

With three minutes left, the other Falcons moved aside and let Kyle handle the ball every time we had it. I was certain that it would take a miracle for him to win this game for us, and I didn't know if we had another miracle left.

This wasn't the kind of basketball I really liked or appreciated, but it was entertaining. During those last three minutes, it came to me as I sat there and watched Kyle run and shoot that the crowd liked the frenzy of the game more than anything else, perhaps even more than winning itself. These normally quiet people liked the chance to scream and stomp their feet for a while each week during the long winter on the reservation; they liked to give vent to the things that they kept inside the rest of the time. Perhaps basketball, in its own way, had become a kind of catharsis and healing ritual—not just in Whiteriver, but in many other places as well.

One thing was undeniable: The local people clearly enjoyed getting excited and—win or lose—showering as much love as they could on their players.

Kyle made a basket to close the gap to 47–40. He hit two more shots to make it 49–45. When he was moving down the court with the ball at full speed, anything seemed possible.

A Round Valley player stole the ball and started down the court by himself. Willie took off after him and caught up just under our goal, tomahawking him for a hard but clean foul. The boy made the basket and a free throw, causing the crowd to moan and to sense, finally, that the game had slipped out of reach.

With thirteen seconds left, Kyle hit a three-pointer, but that was all he could muster. The game ended 52–48, and I wondered as I walked back to the locker room if this were going to be the season we went to the state tournament and won it all. We had a lot of guts and a lot of potential, but having potential in the world of sports means that you haven't fulfilled it yet.

The most unusual thing in athletics is not finding gifted players; they are everywhere across the country. It's finding someone who can reach his full potential. The NBA, not to mention the high school and college ranks, is crowded with guys who don't give all they have on the court each night. We don't just respond to great athletes because they're great but because they push themselves to be greater. In the process, they discover new things about themselves and human limitations. They take us where we haven't yet gone.

When I got to the locker room and looked around at the dejected expressions on the kids' faces—faces that had been so happy a few nights earlier when we'd beaten Blueridge—I told myself that maybe I was wrong. This team was full of surprises, and just when you felt they were going to lose, they sometimes found a way to win.

I was learning what it was really like to coach, to sit on the bench and know that the game was in their hands and not yours. It was like being a parent, and I was starting to think of these guys not just as basketball players, but as members of my own family, my own sons or nephews.

You had to learn to let your children stumble and find their own way, and that was never easy.

— XXIV —

IN JANUARY I LECTURED TO A CLASS OF AROUND
thirty students at Alchesay High. Taught by Joyce Bahe and
Cindy Jackinsky, the class was designed to inform the kids
about the Apache language and culture. Earlier in the decade,
Edgar Perry had started the push in Whiteriver to rekindle interest in the ancient tongue by putting together an Apache dictionary. Becoming familiar with the old language, he believed, was
crucial. Without an attachment to the speech of their ancestors,
the kids today would not know their roots or have a strong identity as Native Americans. They would not know how to venture
out into the larger world without losing their identity and would
be much more likely to retreat back home without getting an
education or some training that would allow them to help their
own people.

Teaching the Apache history and language on the reservation
was a challenge on every level. As in other minority cultures,
many young people in the White Mountain tribe seemed mostly
interested in copying the styles and tastes of mainstream American culture. They listened to popular music by white or African-
American groups and dressed like other kids around the country, in baggy jeans and tennis shoes and jackets. They imitated
the teenage hairdos you saw everywhere, the rattails and buzz-

cuts and other styles that were all over the malls. During the noon hour, they streamed down to Basha's market, a block or so away from the high school, where they lined up in front of the fried food counter or the pastry display and ate things that weren't good for them while reading chic fashion magazines or the *National Enquirer* at the checkout line. They seemed cut off from their roots.

At the same time, many of them had come to Ms. Bahe and Ms. Jackinsky's class wanting to know more about their heritage. In the first weeks of the course, the women had taught them about the clans and subclans that make up the tribe. (Most of the students barely knew about the existence of these clans.) The teachers encouraged them to go home and talk to their parents, grandparents, aunts, uncles, and other family members so they could hear about and absorb the rich oral tradition of their people. They could learn the history and secrets of the clans to which they belonged. Ms. Bahe and Ms. Jackinsky also taught them their genealogy, and the kids drew up elaborate family trees. They brought in old photos of their ancestors and wrote out their names in Apache. They studied the past hundred years on the reservation.

The women taught them about the Great Seal of the White Mountain Apache and why this visual symbol is so important to the tribe. The seal is a circle with a black background and many colorful markings. Its themes originated in the deep past and it now represents the tribe's mythological structure.

The black background stands for the eternity of darkness before time began and the Creator of Life gave light and breath to the Apache. The Creator then blessed the tribe with water, depicted on the seal as snow on Mount Baldy, the tribe's sacred peak. Mount Baldy and the other White Mountains scattered across the reservation hold the game—the deer, pheasants, turkey, bear, wild pigs, and smaller animals that have been hunted by the Apache for centuries—symbolized on the seal by a huge elk. An evergreen tree stands for the tribe's abundant forest resources and a rainbow arching over the mountains represents the hope for peace.

The round wickiup on the seal symbolizes the ancestral abode of the tribe. The small *tus* is a water container, critical for the Apache's survival in the past, made from native reeds and coated with pitch from pinon trees. The seal's four sacred colors—black, blue, yellow, and white—signify the constant movement of the tribe from darkness to light, from dusk to dawn to dusk again. The White Mountain Apache give reverence to this never ending cycle of life. It has guided them in their prayers to the Creator.

Two lightning bolts on the seal are also sacred symbols. During the most significant of all the tribe's dances—the Crown Dance—the men put on a crown bedecked with the feathers of an eagle, worshiped because it flies higher than other birds. The men paint lightning bolts on their flesh. Dancers who have gone up to Mount Baldy and been instructed by mysterious mountain spirits then enact healing rituals for the White Mountain Apache in a dance that's still performed today.

Apache kids, like so many others, often know little about their tribe's underlying values and belief system, their core myth. The Great Seal generates tremendous interest among the Alchesay High students because it's the living image of the ideas and faith the tribe has lived by for longer than anyone can remember. It's the visible emblem of what they've brought forward from the past—and of their connection to what remains invisible but present in their own lives, handed down through centuries of endurance.

Ms. Bahe and Ms. Jackinsky instruct the kids on how to pronounce in Apache the names of everything shown on the seal. They also teach them Apache words that express basic emotions such as happy, sad, and angry. They teach them the names of body parts, animals, foods, the months of the year, and the various subcommunities within Whiteriver. They demonstrate how to utilize the Apache dictionary and put words together in sentences. It's a slow and awkward process, but gradually the language is being revitalized in school classrooms and across the reservation.

"We want them to be proud of being Apache and to know why they should be proud of their heritage," says Cindy Jackinsky. "Our class gives them a basic appreciation of their culture, which has been lacking in the past. Many of the students don't know anything about that culture or the history of the clans or where they came from. They don't have any sense of being connected to their past.

"We've asked them to do research on their clans and have found that many of their parents have also come in because they want to know more about their own backgrounds. They want to understand the Great Seal and why it's significant in their lives today. They're looking for meaning in these things, and we're filling in some of the gaps.

"The kids often tell us that without the Apache language they are no longer Apache, so we must keep them speaking it."

■⟍⟍⟍⟍■ I ARRIVED FOR MY LECTURE AT 1:15 P.M. IT WAS held in a makeshift classroom in a trailerlike structure at the rear of the school. Next to this building was a greenhouse with a picture of a Native American painted on its side along with the words "Geronimo's Garden." Inside the trailer, kids were sitting in rows of chairs and it was quite warm. On the wall was a sign that read, "Joy and pain live in the same house."

I opened the lecture by telling them that African Americans, like Native Americans, had been in this country for much longer than was generally recognized and for far longer than their white counterparts who had landed on Plymouth Rock. Back in 1513, Balboa, who discovered the Pacific Ocean, had found Africans on the Isthmus of Panama, at least fifty years before the slave trade had begun in America. And Native Americans had been living here centuries before that.

Both groups, I told the class, had been held in slavery, and Native Americans had been treated just as badly as African Americans. Our peoples had a deep and complex past together. We had often been allies in horrible circumstances and we had also been adversaries, but many of these events have not been written in the history books used by schools. I gave them half a dozen examples of such omissions:

—In 1527 the slave trade to Mexico had to be stopped when an insurrection of blacks and Indians, fighting together, overwhelmed the military garrison protecting Mexico City. The escapees were never seen again.

—In 1570 the Viceroy Martin Enriquez made a policy decision to separate Indians and blacks, because once again they were planning uprisings to free themselves.

—In 1780 Ottowa Indians helped many escaping African-American slaves flee to Canada.

—Unlike the Ottowa, the Creek, Choctaw, and Chickasaw tribes had all been slaveholders.

—In 1843 the Seminole Indians and African Americans had fought two wars with the U.S. government in order to maintain their independence in north-central Florida.

—The first non–Native American to explore the Southwest was an African slave named Estevanico. He accompanied the Narvaez expedition in its attempt to map the coastline along the Gulf of Mexico. It was his stories about the "Seven Cities of Gold" that fueled the greed that eventually led to the Spanish domination of the area.

African Americans and Native Americans, I told the students, shared a common history of oppression. The Spanish had enslaved Indians and made them work in the mines in Sonora. Yet in some ways the Native American experience was very different from my own ancestors'. Blacks had been removed from their homeland and taken elsewhere. After centuries of abuse and things worse than abuse, we were getting the education and skills needed to wield economic and political power in a modern society.

The White Mountain Apache had kept their land but had not been taught many of the skills necessary to cope with and compete in contemporary American life. They had not, until very recently, been taught that knowledge is a tool and a way out of their circumstances. It is a critical tool that does not belong to any one group of people. Knowledge is available to everyone who is willing to work for it. It's a lot like electricity, as I'd tried to explain to minority kids in other places; it is just something to be used to help yourself change your reality.

I shared with them the story of the Buffalo Soldiers and John Glass and his duties as chief scout at Fort Apache. I described how the Buffalo Soldiers and the White Mountain Apache, working in cooperation and risking their lives together in dangerous terrain, had captured a hostile Apache leader named Mangas, the only time a renegade Apache was ever taken captive under arms.

As I looked out over the class and spoke these words, I realized that some of the kids sitting in front of me were direct descendants of the people John Glass had ridden with back in the 1880s. I was standing not far from where these White Mountain Apache and African Americans had stood together more than a century ago, handing down stories from our past. There was a picture of Lieutenant Thomas B. Gatewood on the wall of the classroom. Lt. Gatewood had been stationed at Fort Apache and had finally gotten Geronimo to surrender. I had Gatewood's uniform insignia with me and showed it to the kids, who were very excited to see and touch it. More circles were being closed.

After I finished the lecture, the students asked questions and then left their seats and came forward to examine some photos I'd brought in of Glass and other nineteenth-century figures.

They held the pictures and looked at them intensely. They seemed fascinated that all of these things had unfolded so long before they were born, amazed that their history, in its own way, kept repeating itself with new people and new opportunities.

Lecturing to them about the long-ago interaction of Native Americans and African Americans was a lot like coaching basketball on the reservation. In the time that was available, I could only touch the surface of many things. I couldn't go as far as I wanted to, couldn't really lecture in depth, just as I couldn't break many of the Falcons' bad habits on the court, but I could encourage them to explore new things and improve their own condition. I could polish them a little and give them some guidelines for the future, point them in a different direction so that if they wanted to help themselves, they at least knew where to begin.

THE STUDENTS in Ms. Bahe and Ms. Jackinsky's class were mostly too young to understand what I was saying about the historical ties between Native Americans and African Americans, or why I felt such things were important, or how these things might affect their lives some day. The kids seemed most interested in the pictures of my own family that I'd brought with me to the class. These were still teenagers who were just learning to stretch their muscles, form their own identities, and ask their own questions.

Years or even decades might pass before some of them really thought about their backgrounds or what their ancestors had achieved or what had been stripped away from them after the U.S. military arrived. I couldn't accomplish all that I wanted to in one lecture or one basketball season on the reservation. The past was too big and pervasive for that. But I could let them know that they came from a great historical tradition, as rich and meaningful as anyone's, and from a people who had survived brutally difficult times and the constant insults of the dominant culture. Not so long ago, signs in Globe, Arizona, had read, "No dogs, no Apache."

Their tribe had never been conquered or defeated. I was here to remind them of that. I couldn't know exactly what they were getting from my visit, but this experience was a privilege for me.

— XXVI —

THE REGULAR SEASON WENT ALONG PRETTY much as it had so far. We played well for a while, then faltered, and then repeated this pattern. We were practicing much better than we had been back in November, and we strived for consistency in our games, but it remained elusive. Some nights I thought we were genuinely improving and were going to play our best basketball of the year at precisely the right time, when the regional and state tournaments came around in early February, but other nights I couldn't help seeing the big holes that were still in our game. We continued to make too many mistakes and didn't use our big men enough when the contest was on the line.

Yet there were many good signs. For the last ten games of the regular season, Willie became a starter and kept improving. Ivan was also working his way into the starting lineup and would crack it the final game before the tournaments began. He was playing much stickier defense and rebounding better than only a few months earlier. He may even have been jumping a little higher in order to keep up with Willie.

Ivan presented my greatest psychological challenge as a coach, and he had a breakthrough late in the season. He had learned to do something difficult but critical for an athlete: He was now playing through his periods of frustration rather than just quitting and standing around on the court with a far-off expression in his eyes, like a child who's retreated so deep within himself that he cannot be reached.

Basketball is a game that flows. It flows toward you and it flows away from you. If you stay focused and continue playing hard, no matter how badly things are going, the flow eventually changes and moves back toward you. It's only when you quit that you fall out of the flow. Players don't really believe all this until they've proven it to themselves. Then they think it's magic.

Ivan had stayed with himself and his game long enough to see results. One time I even found him in the gym alone doing the "George Mikan" drill, which I'd been showing him and Willie and Butter throughout the season. He was standing on the court shooting the ball off the backboard with his right and then his left hand, one hand right after the other in rapid succession, and many of his shots were going in. This was the kind of thing that would not show up in the box score of a particular game or perhaps even in the season's final record, but it was progress.

Sometimes I felt that my greatest achievement with the team was getting them to understand the difference between good criticism from a coach and getting their feelings hurt by an adult. It had taken me quite a while to grasp that the White Mountain Apache really do have serious issues around performance anxiety and don't like being singled out and put in the spotlight, especially a negative spotlight. The players tended to see their mistakes—or having someone point out their mistakes—as something to be ashamed of instead of just part of the process of growing and learning.

I never completely broke through this cultural barrier, and it remained an underlying theme throughout the season. But I do think I got some of the guys to see that the only way to get better at basketball or other things is by acknowledging and confronting what you don't know—and always being willing to change. My job involved a lot of subtle battles; even the smallest of victories felt good.

Like Ivan, Don Ray Johnson just kept coming on. When the season had begun, I'd mostly viewed him as a roughneck with a penchant for fighting, but he had dedicated himself at practice and improved dramatically over the months. With more minutes on the floor, who knows what he could have done?

Tony was gradually playing more under control, but there was still an edge to his game and his personality. The last act between us had not yet been played out, but it would soon unfold on the basketball floor.

As the season wore on, Butter had returned to the safety of his comfort zone, which was standing outside and shooting his fadeaway jump shot instead of venturing inside and using his bulk against our larger opponents. It wasn't so much the contact he was afraid of but his fear that he could not get off the ground. Sometimes you have to forget your weaknesses and just play. You have to convince yourself that you're bigger than you are.

Loren's problem was different from Butter's. He was what is known in basketball as a "tweener"—a player who is between sizes. Quick and agile, he wasn't quite big enough to go down low and wasn't a true perimeter player, either. He was caught between two positions, but he always worked hard in the games.

Joe Parker, on the other hand, was a true guard. He was one of our best outside shooters and was now giving us some good minutes, along with Blaine and Orlando and Tinker Burnette, our other good shooter from the outside.

My favorite memory of Blaine came one day at practice when Kyle was working on something at the far end of the court and went down with a minor injury. Blaine immediately stopped our drill and instinctively moved toward his older sibling.

Kyle was already getting up off the floor and was clearly going to be all right. I told Blaine to come back and resume doing the drill, but he kept walking. He looked over his shoulder at me with an expression of shock and pain on his face.

"But he's my brother," he said. He didn't have to say anything else.

IN MID-JANUARY, we fell into a slump. We lost to Show Low and then St. John's due to some sloppy play. Then we lost again to San Carlos. I was relieved to learn that the folks at San Carlos didn't want drunks at their games. The handful of people who had harassed me when we'd played San Carlos earlier in Whiteriver were not admitted to this contest.

Willie had a great moment in the San Carlos game—his finest of the year. With only a few minutes left to play, their excellent guard, Alvin Antonio, who'd had an outstanding game against us, grabbed the ball in our end of the court and took off with it toward the basket. Willie chased after him, closing fast. Taking two giant strides at the free throw line, Willie launched himself up and over Alvin's shoulder, stopping the attempted layup in midflight. He didn't just block it. He knocked it ten or twelve rows into the stands and brought the Alchesay fans roaring to their feet, including everyone on the bench.

This was a pure basketball memory, especially for anyone old enough to remember Bill Russell playing defense for the Boston Celtics and dramatically blocking shots against Wilt Chamberlain and the Philadelphia Warriors in their classic matchups during the 1960s. Nobody ever did this better or with more flair than Russell.

For months, I'd coached our big men on defensive maneuvers and how to time their leaps so they would leave the floor at the exact moment to swat away their opponents' shots with maximum impact. I'd told them that if they did this the right way they would see exciting results, but they didn't really believe me.

Now Willie had done it and truly surprised himself. It was the highest I'd ever seen him jump, the highest I think he'd ever been. It was higher than he'd thought he could go. He came down smiling and laughing, realizing that he had more spring in his legs and more talent for the game than he'd ever understood. He could play above the rim now, and he knew it. Basketball is about many things, and one of them is our eternal desire to get off the ground, to get away from gravity for a while and fly. For a couple of great seconds, Willie left the earth behind.

WILLIE'S BLOCK was a highlight in the bumpy road that our season had become. In most games, we'd start off strong, but then mysteriously stop scoring in the second half; we simply could not play four straight good quarters of basketball. After dropping four games in a row, we lost again to Winslow. (Ivan was out sick for this one and Willie wasn't available because of a hurt finger.) It looked as if the whole season were sliding away. Then we beat Holbrook, but we could not get a winning streak going. We lost to Blueridge, then revenged the hard loss to Round Valley by beating them on the road. We lost to Show Low again but beat Hopi, one of our archrivals, and then beat St. John's at home. We flip-flopped the entire second half of the season, losing more games than we won and never putting together good performances back to back.

The team, I'd come to realize, was a lot like the kids in Ms. Bahe and Ms. Jackinsky's Apache language class. They were caught between two cultures, two styles, and two ways of playing basketball. They weren't the same squad they had been last fall when I'd arrived on the reservation, but they weren't exactly the one I'd hoped to help shape during my time in Whiteriver. They were going through a transition period, with one foot in each world, so they were always a little off balance.

They were trying hard to add new things to their old approach to the game but had not yet developed a dependable method of play that carried them through the tough spots. Each time I felt they were about to gell, they stumbled again.

And every time they got in trouble late in the fourth quarter, they let Kyle take over.

DURING THE ST. JOHN'S GAME in Whiteriver, I had a strange and disorienting experience. It crept up on me and was one of those small things that tells you that a lot of years have passed and that you've seen a lot of changes in your lifetime. It happened in the pregame warm-up, while our team was shooting layups and I was half-listening to some rap music on the PA system. It took me a few moments to realize that I was hearing Bugs Bunny do an elaborate rap about basketball—the same number he had performed in the movie *Space Jam*.

I thought back to my childhood memories of Bugs, when he had been a wisecracking cartoon figure in the early days of television. The kids in my neighborhood had always gathered around a TV to laugh at him on Saturday mornings. It was suddenly forty years later: I was no longer a young man, and Bugs was no longer just a funny TV rabbit. He'd become a movie-star rap artist who was talking in rhyme about hoops, speaking the language of the 'hood.

We'd all traveled a long, weird road since my childhood.

IN THE FIRST WEEK of February, we lost for the second time to Snowflake. Before this game, I was given my salary for the season: a Morgan silver dollar from 1878. Superintendent Clark had felt that a dollar from the days of the Buffalo Soldiers was just the thing for me, and as usual, his instincts were right.

We closed out the regular season with a loss to San Carlos. The defeats had piled up, but I wasn't too discouraged. I still felt that we were expanding our game and might surpass everyone when the tournaments started.

BY THE END of the regular season, I had grown close enough to the team to regard it as part of my extended family. As in families everywhere, conflict is occasionally inevitable.

One night after a game, Coach Mendoza and I were in the locker room, and I was getting ready to leave. I'd finished up all my duties with the guys and was about to drive back to the condo when Mendoza asked me for some more autographs for his relatives, acquaintances, and friends. He'd been doing this for weeks, and I'd been steadily signing the pieces of paper he brought to me. Now I was tired of this—and just plain tired. He could have made the request earlier in the evening when I was fresher and would have taken care of it, but this was not the right moment. The game had been draining, and I had thirty miles of night driving ahead of me. I wanted to go home and get some rest.

Tension had been building over this issue for some time, and I'd hoped the situation wouldn't come to a showdown, but now I had to deal with it.

Autographs are one of the curses of modern celebrity. It was bad enough back in the old days when people would interrupt you at any moment—in a restaurant, at a movie, or when just walking down the street—to ask you to sign something for them because they wanted it for themselves or their children. I always hoped that what people had carried away from my days as a performer were good and vivid memories, so they didn't really need anything more than that. Besides, your name scribbled on a piece of paper really wasn't worth that much. Today, all that has changed, and there's a thriving market for celebrity autographs, not to mention another thriving market for forged signatures. Now your life is not only interrupted by strangers who claim to want something for themselves or a relative, but by people who want to buy or sell a piece of your handwriting. Even that has become a commodity.

If you always say yes to the autograph seekers, you will never stop signing the things that are shoved at you. If you say no, you're labeled as a bad or difficult person. It's a dilemma with no easy answer. I grew up as an only child who spent many hours alone in his room reading and thinking. As an adult, I have never, because of my size, been able to hide in public. I'm an individual who has always needed to spend time alone and be left alone when I need to be alone. Because of this, I've been called moody and distant and uncaring and unreachable, but it's only by being alone that I can discover who I am and live the life I want to lead.

I don't act the way I do to shut others out, unless I believe they need to be shut out. I act this way in order to manage myself the best way I know how. I find balance by going within and exploring what is there. It all sounds simple, but when you're over seven feet tall and well-known, it quickly becomes much more complicated.

I have always expected people to understand that there are limitations to what you can reasonably demand of celebrities in public settings, but many don't understand this. They will take from you as long as you let them. They will not recognize that you are just a human being who happens to have a special talent or gift. Sooner or later you have to set boundaries and make things clear, and that can be unpleasant. Coach Mendoza was not always clear about boundaries, either at practice or off the court. I had not wanted the situation with him to reach this point, but now it had, and something needed to be said.

I told him that I'd signed enough autographs for him, and I wouldn't be signing any more.

That was all it took.

He quickly understood and apologized. We never had to discuss it again.

IN LATE JANUARY I RECEIVED THE MARTIN LUTHER King Award from Arizona State University in Tempe. ASU had been instrumental in getting Arizona to recognize Dr. King's birthday as a holiday—one of two states that had officially adopted this as a holiday by popular vote—despite some local opposition to the idea. I told the gathering in Tempe that I was sorry that Arizona, which was filled with good people, had elected Governor Evan Meacham a few years back, but that I was also proud of the state for later impeaching him for his misbehavior. Anybody can make a mistake; it's how you deal with it that counts. They had dealt with this one well.

I also said that one of the best things about my coaching experience in Whiteriver was getting to see and explore more of their state. I had always felt that California was easily the most beautiful state in the country, but after spending several months in Arizona, I was beginning to change my mind. The Western landscape and wide-open vistas around Whiteriver, the sprawling ponderosa pine forests on the reservation, the mountains and mesas and high-country meadows, the big game and blue sky and clear light, the canyons and the horizons stretching out in every direction—all of these things were working their way into me and giving me a greater appreciation of their land.

It carried with it a sense of history and freedom and endless possibilities. In Arizona you not only felt that you could start over and leave the past behind, but you could also live the life you'd dreamed of as a boy in New York City.

THE REGIONAL TOURNAMENT began in Whiteriver in the second week of February. Our first game was against Holbrook, and we came out playing great. Everything we had been working on at practice throughout the season gelled, and we went up by 18 points at the half. It was our best performance of the season.

We moved the ball into Ivan and Willie in the pivot; Kyle and Tony put up good outside shots and they were falling. Our defense was tight and our turnovers were way down. We were playing physically but under control. I began to feel that all of my effort to teach the kids was paying off and that they had absorbed much of what I had to offer. The guys weren't merely showing some real potential this evening, they were fulfilling it on the court. This was very gratifying for me—but the moment wasn't to last.

Our worst enemy, inconsistency, was lurking nearby and ready to invade. In the second half, Holbrook came rushing back, mostly by hitting their three-point shots. Our offensive production slowed way down and almost stopped, which had been our problem throughout the last part of the season. We could play a good half, but not a whole game—as if the team were still only halfway to where it wanted to be.

Holbrook immediately sensed this and took advantage of it. The more passively we played, the more aggressive their players became. Now my feelings about the Falcons swung in the opposite direction, and I had the yo-yo emotional experience of wondering why my team had disappeared. Our guys weren't doing anything we'd told them to do. They seemed to have forgotten how to play. The game was turning, but there wasn't much I could do except sit back and watch, hoping that our lead was big enough to escape with a win. If we couldn't, our season would end right here, and that would be a terrible disappointment after going to the state tournament last year and losing the championship game by only three points.

In the fourth quarter, we awakened and returned to form. The strange thing that accompanies and runs underneath all basketball games—that elusive "energy flow"—started moving our way again. Our shots began falling and we hung on to defeat Holbrook.

The next game was against St. John's. With an excellent effort from Willie, Ivan, and our guards, we beat them and were now qualified to play the next round of the regional tourney in Winslow. It would be against our season-long nemesis, Snowflake. They'd already defeated us twice this year, and both losses had been hard to accept. I was convinced that we were a better team, yet we hadn't shown it. Maybe now we could, especially after the rousing victory against St. John's.

Before the Snowflake game, something happened at practice, something that, when I look back, seemed almost inevitable. It had been building ever since I'd arrived in Whiteriver and had been at the edges of our workouts and games once the season had started. Maybe it was something that finally had to come out so we could all get on with the business of learning.

As with my conflict over the autograph signing with Coach Mendoza, I hadn't really wanted to deal with this one head-on either, but sometimes that's the only choice left.

— XXVIII —

THROUGHOUT THE SEASON, SHASHEEN PARKER had labored diligently as the team's student manager. She had always been there when she was supposed to be and had taken care of some of the travel plans and equipment details for the Falcons. Her job involved a lot of grunt work, but she hadn't complained about it. She'd been excellent during the 1998–99 campaign and was a valuable asset to the club.

Shasheen was also a teenage girl who was constantly around the teenage boys on the team. That made her position more challenging, but she had handled herself well. In addition to all of these things, she was Tony Parker's cousin, Tommy Parker's daughter, and Joe Parker's sister. She was obviously quite familiar with these relatives, but she was also close with everyone on the squad. The guys often horsed around with her and teased her, but none of this had ever gotten out of hand—until state tournament time.

After beating St. John's, we scheduled a practice for the next day. Before it began, several players were out on the court warming up while Shasheen was watching them and performing some of her tasks. I was there, because I always got to practice early to get in some jumping with my heavy rope, but Coach Mendoza had not yet shown up. Tony had been shooting around and poking fun at Shasheen. They'd been talking back and forth, but this went on all the time.

Tony suddenly rushed toward her and picked her up, throwing her over his shoulder and twirling her around.

I let go of my jump rope and asked him to put her down. He didn't pay any attention to me.

She began to yell and screech, partly out of surprise, partly out of fear, and partly because he was holding her in such a way that she was helpless, unable to get free.

"Let her go," I said to Tony. He ignored me.

She was still shouting as I came toward them.

The other players had stopped shooting and gathered around the action, staring at us. I hadn't known if they'd sensed the underlying drama that had existed between Tony and me since last November. Now they didn't have to sense it. It was coming to a head—out in the open on the court.

The gym had fallen silent, and Shasheen's voice was now barely audible.

"Put her down," I said once more, coming closer to Tony and his cousin.

He didn't do as I asked.

Many young men have tried to force their will on women and others through physical intimidation, and athletes have figured prominently in some of these situations. It was important for me that Tony understood this wasn't going to be allowed. I have martial arts training and sometimes it comes in handy.

With no alternatives left, I grabbed him and pinched the fronts of his biceps with enough force to cause discomfort and make him quickly put her down.

Shasheen walked away. I was relieved, thinking the confrontation was over.

Tony wheeled toward me, lowered his head, and drove his shoulder straight into me, pushing me backward and down to the floor on my back. Besides being a good basketball guard, he was also a talented football player who knew how to tackle.

Before he could get away, I grabbed his shirt and held him down with me on the floor. As he tried to free himself, I stood and was able to take control of one of Tony's legs and keep him from moving. At this point, it had stopped being fun for Tony, and he knew where things were going. I raised his leg until he fell to the court, and then I used my weight to pin him on his back with my forearm across his throat.

The others players had been watching all this, speechless. Now Willie came up to us and kneeled down and began to count over Tony, as if he were a referee in a wrestling match. He was counting Tony out. It was a much-needed attempt at humor in a situation that was no longer funny.

When Willie stopped counting, I let Tony up, shocked by what he'd done. Throughout twenty years in pro basketball nobody had ever tackled me on the court.

He could have injured me and I could have injured him. If he'd caused physical harm to anyone, he could have been suspended from the team, which would have hurt the Falcons' chances in the tournament. I was grateful that my martial arts background had enabled me to take contol without anyone getting hurt or suspended. The only damage had been to my reading glasses—and a little blood on Tony's teeth.

Whatever had been building within Tony over the past few

months was now out. He resumed his practice warm-up that after-noon as if nothing had happened. We didn't interact much the rest of the day, and I was trying to decide what to do or say next.

I didn't want to make trouble for Tony, so I chose to let it go and hoped that he had learned his lesson. The next day I heard that he'd been going around the school telling kids that he'd gotten the better of me in the incident and pinned me to the gym floor. Rick Sanchez told me that Tony was trying to spin the story his way instead of confronting what had really taken place on the court, and that was unacceptable.

That evening we played Snowflake in Winslow. Before the game, Joe Parker was messing around with Shasheen when he grabbed her neck and shoulders and wouldn't let go. This was his sister, and he had probably been doing this kind of thing at home for years, but I got right on him, and he took his hands off her neck as if they'd been burned.

I called the team together and told them that Shasheen was our manager and deserved our respect for the fine job she'd done for us all year. Then I paused and looked around the room, settling my eyes first on Joe and then on Tony.

"If any of you guys don't want to give her that respect or treat her right," I said, "you're going to have to deal with me. Do you understand that?"

No one spoke up.

"Do you want to deal with me?" I asked.

A couple of the kids mumbled no or shook their heads. Tony and Joe held their silence.

Nobody else picked Shasheen up or mistreated her the rest of the season. Fortunately for everyone, I know the difference between mischief and evil.

▓▓▓▓▓ **IN THE NEXT ROUND OF THE REGIONAL TOURNAMENT,** we lost to Snowflake. It was the third time this year that they'd beaten us, although I'd always felt that we had the better team. They were bigger than we were—the problem we could not solve—and they controlled the rebounding and much of the inside play. It was a tough loss, but because of the complicated structure of the Arizona high school tourney, our season was still alive.

Our first two wins had already qualified us for the state tournament and we now traveled to Winslow—to play against Winslow in the first round of the state. We'd beaten them on the road in the regular season, so we were confident about traveling to their gym and challenging them there—perhaps too confident. We played hard but lost again. Our season-long problem—inconsistency—was still controlling our game and cost us this one. In sports terminology, winning is mostly about execution, about doing the right things when they count the most, and we simply weren't able to do that.

During the regional and state tournaments, I experienced what coaches go through at the high school, college, and pro level when not only individual games but their jobs or careers may be at stake. There is almost always a gap between what you know your team can do—what you've seen them do in practice—and how they perform on the court under pressure. Coaches tend to live in that gap, in that place where their vision of what their team is capable of is in conflict with the reality of what's happening on the floor. Living there can be maddening and make them seem a little crazed during tournaments or the playoffs. I'd never gone through this before on the bench and could feel what it might do to someone's stomach. During our losses to Snowflake and Winslow, Coach Mendoza, Rick, Tommy, and I traded a lot of head-shaking and pained expressions, but none of us could put on a uniform or make the kids do what we wanted them to do.

A few nights after these two defeats, on February 16, we had one more shot to stay in the tourney, playing against Ganado in Flagstaff. If we lost this time, the season was over. We were taller than Ganado, the only game in which this had been true all year long, and our big men dominated theirs. Ivan and Willie were terrific, and the Falcons led most of the way. Tonight, they were fulfilling our vision of them as a team and closing that gap.

Since Tony and I had had our tiff a few days earlier, he had been performing better than ever, as if something had finally passed from his system and he was now able to stop worrying and start focusing on improving his game. His physical skills had always been there, but he hadn't learned how to think through basketball and he'd just continued making too many mistakes. That was starting to change, and he was finally bringing together the mental part of the game with what his body was capable of. I went up to him before the Ganado game and said just one thing: "Take an extra moment to think before acting." He was superb that night, hitting his shots, playing good defense, and not throwing the ball away, giving us one of his best efforts of the season.

We were ahead all the way until late in the fourth quarter, when Ganado began to catch up, steadily eating away at our lead. Our season had been shaped by two baffling patterns that we'd never really been able to break: getting so far behind that we couldn't come back or getting far ahead but not being able to maintain a lead. The latter took over now, and I sat on the bench next to Tommy, where we both squirmed and groaned as Ganado got back into the game.

As often happens when a team loses focus and momentum shifts, the calls started going against us. (Officials feel and respond to the flow of the action, too.) One of the refs made a bad call against the Falcons and then another referee made a second call that was downright horrible. The first one was fairly understandable: It was a foul on Tinker after he had leaped up and cleanly blocked a shot, but the ref saw it differently.

Ganado made their free throws and tied the game with less than a minute left to play.

Our fans were on their feet and screaming, as they had been throughout the year. They were sending out whistles and war cries, jumping up and down and begging our kids to extend their season by at least one more game. Everyone on the team and everyone in Whiteriver wanted to see the Falcons return to the state championship finals at the America West Arena in Phoenix. Capturing the state title was obviously important, but getting there was perhaps just as important, because it would give the guys the chance to visit a place where pro basketball was played, and that was something they would remember—win or lose—for the rest of their lives. I wanted to be with them and see the pride on their faces when they took the court in Phoenix. It was what I had been looking forward to all year long.

We inbounded the ball, came down the floor, and made several passes. Then Kyle put up a shot that fell in, giving us a 2-point lead with only five seconds left. Our fans were stomping and roaring behind me, the coaches were up, and we were lifting our hands in the air, waving them, telling the kids not to foul or make any other mistakes and we could escape from Flagstaff with a win.

A Ganado player threw the ball in and we intercepted it for a steal. We now had the ball and a lead and everyone on our side let out a huge breath of relief. The game was ours.

As we prepared to toss the ball in and run out the clock, one of the officials stopped play and said that Ganado had called a time-out before trying to inbound the ball. Because of this, our steal didn't count, and they would get to bring the ball in again. It was a terrible ruling, one of the worst I've ever seen in these circumstances at the end of a game.

Our fans went wild, not believing what they'd just seen. They booed and howled with indignation. They kicked and wailed and turned away from the floor in disgust. Ten seconds earlier, they'd been preparing to enjoy the victory and now they were stunned by the thought that the game had not been decided. The gym was full of powerfully swinging emotions.

I was up and shouting at the refs, too, the first time I'd really cut loose since taking off my glasses and handing them to an official back in Tucson against Cholla in the first month of the season. This evening, I felt there was nothing to lose and I might as well vent what I was feeling. You never want the outcome of a crucial game to turn on an official's call, particularly when four months of hard work and your whole season hangs in the balance. As I stood by the bench and booed, I realized how close to the kids I'd gotten since last November and how much I wanted them to win. I wanted it for them—and for me.

If they lost, it suddenly hit me, as it had before in recent weeks, my time on the reservation would be over. I didn't want that to happen, not yet anyway. Not tonight. The months had gone by too quickly and I hadn't done everything I'd wanted to do. I'd hoped to have more time to ride horses and go skiing. I wanted to get to know the kids and their families better, and I wanted to teach them more things, both on the court and off. I wanted to give them more, but now . . .

We brought the guys over to the sidelines to settle them down and get them ready for the last five ticks on the clock. Their faces were already filled with disappointment. Just moments ago, they'd felt that they'd won the game, which is a dangerous thing for any team to feel until time has completely run out. We reminded them that they were still ahead by two points, and we told them to put the bad call behind them and focus. All they had to do was make one more defensive stand and then they could celebrate.

They nodded as if they wanted to believe us and went back onto the floor, but their bodies were dragging and they looked uncertain.

Ganado inbounded and one of their guards brought the ball upcourt, driving toward our basket. When he was about twenty-five feet from the goal, the clock was almost at zero, so he stopped and raised the ball to his chest with both hands. He let it fly, tossing up a shot that can best be described as very low percentage. The chances of its going in may have been one in ten, or one in twenty or thirty.

It floated toward the basket and all of us, everybody inside the gymnasium, followed it as it fell toward the rim. Time ran out and the buzzer sounded as it passed through the net—good for three points and a stunning win for Ganado.

On their bench, the shot unleashed total chaotic joy. Their substitutes and fans and cheerleaders ran out onto the floor and buried their players in a huge tumbling mass of happy teenagers.

The Falcons stood and stared, hands on hips and eyes wide with shock. After each of our games, players from both teams were supposed to line up and shake hands in a long row, as they do in hockey after a playoff series has come to an end, but that was impossible in these conditions. Their kids were mobbing one another at one end of the court and our players, except for Butter, were now wandering around in a daze or numbly making their way back to our locker room. Their season had come to a halt in one moment, and it had happened so fast that none of us could quite grasp the finality of this game.

Our year was finished. We would never come together in this way again and I felt empty.

Butter was lying on his back in the middle of the court with his hands rolled into fists. His fists were covering his eyes and he was writhing on the floor and crying like a small boy. I spotted him and immediately walked toward him, as if I didn't have any choice in the matter. When I reached him, I bent down and held his arm and whispered in his ear. My words came from more than four decades of playing competitive sports and winning and losing many different games in front of the public.

"Not here, Butter," I said.

He gazed up at me.

"Not here," I said again.

He nodded as if he understood. I helped pull him to his feet.

We made our way through the crowd and into the locker room, where Coach Mendoza had gathered the kids around him and wanted to say a few things. There were tears in many people's eyes and some of the kids were angry with themselves for letting the game slip away.

In his soft voice, Mendoza talked about the things that no one wants to hear right after a devastating loss, but they were basically true things and needed to be underlined now that the basketball year had been completed at Alchesay High for 1998–99. They were the things that might echo in the kids' heads long after they left Flagstaff and their school days behind.

"People didn't expect much from us this season," he said. "They didn't think we'd get this far. They didn't pick us to even make it to the state tournament. But we did make it here, and we played hard, and we accomplished a lot. It was a good year and we'll be back next season and go further."

Butter was still crying and the other kids were sitting around half-dressed, looking glum.

It was far too early for them to realize that they'd learned a lot this season and that maybe what they'd learned would help them in the future. I thought about saying something like this but then decided against it. They would make certain discoveries on their own, in their own time and in their own way.

I didn't make a speech, but asked if they would be holding a team meeting the next day, where we might all get together and say a final good-bye. This question bounced around the room, but no one, including the coaches, was sure what was going to take place tomorrow, so I said good-byes to the players and coaches and then left the locker room, ready to go back to my hotel.

Tony's parents, who are separated, were waiting for me outside the locker room and walked up to me at the doorway. I wasn't sure what they wanted and, given my history with their son, I was a little apprehensive.

They both smiled and stuck out their hands to shake mine. I took them, feeling relieved and pleased. They graciously thanked me for the job I'd done with Tony this year and said how much they appreciated my spending the season with the team. We took some pictures together, with Tony's toddler niece, Darieus Parker, included in the photograph. Ever since last November, the little girl had cried and run away each time I'd come near her, but tonight she smiled for the camera.

I told Tony's parents that it meant a lot to me to receive their thanks. I said their son had a future in basketball and could probably get a scholarship to play at a small college. He should go on, I told them, with both the game and his education, and one day he could be a leader in their community.

They thanked me again and I left the building, walking out into the chilly night and feeling that there were more important things than losing to Ganado.

— XXX —

EARLY THE NEXT MORNING, I LEFT FLAGSTAFF
and drove the Expedition back to Lakeside. I stopped at the
condo and packed my things, then drove on down to Whiteriver
and parked at the high school. Unfortunately, John Clark was
not there that day, so I could not thank him for inviting me to
the reservation or say good-bye to him in person. I was sorry to
have missed the opportunity.

Along with Edgar Perry, John was most responsible for bringing me to Whiteriver and giving me the chance to coach the
Falcons. He had opened a new door for me and helped widen
both my sense of involvement with kids and my sense of family.
His affection for and commitment to the White Mountain Apache
tribe was something that was cause for hope. As he'd once put
it, without the bonds of family, the reservation could be a bleak
place, but those bonds were tight and he was a part of them.

Everyone who came to the reservation, regardless of his or
her skin color, age, sex, or belief system, everyone who jour-
neyed here and mingled with the people, everyone who moved
past the stereotypes we hold so easily of others, was a piece of
that large family.

Clark was out that morning, but I found his secretary, Doreen,
and gave her my set of keys to the gym. I thanked her for all

her help during the past four months and got back into my Expedition.

I headed south on Highway 73, moving through the dry landscape of central Arizona, which that winter had been even drier than usual. There had been almost no snow since my arrival. The land was all beige and brown, crackling underfoot when you walked across it and looking as if it could easily catch fire. The biggest snowfall of the year would come on April 1.

I drove and thought about the kids, already missing them and wondering how they were recovering from the night before. I couldn't believe the season had disappeared so quickly and that I wouldn't be coaching them again. But I had my memories and mementos.

From a small bag, I took out something I'd been given, a turquoise belt buckle, and placed it on the seat next to me. I glanced down at it as I steered the vehicle across the narrow roads. One evening, I'd had dinner with Kyle and Blaine Goklish and their parents, the Alsenays, at their home. It had been a wonderful, celebratory occasion. We'd laughed about many things inside the warmth and hospitality of their house— about the eccentricities of some of the people on the reservation and some of the underlying battles that go on in a town where many citizens are Christian but many others hold traditional Apache beliefs. Both groups may be praying to the same god, but each one thinks the other group is trying to harm them and looks for ways to escape the trouble that may be coming. I laughed and felt accepted and happy eating at the Goklish table.

That evening, Kyle gave me a beautiful turquoise belt buckle made of small beads. Its background was the same color as the blue trims on the Alchesay basketball uniforms, and it featured the image of a bird made out of yellow beads. The bird was supposed to be a falcon, but I told Kyle that while the buckle was very handsome, someone had made a mistake, because the bird was modeled on a bald eagle rather than anything else. We laughed about that, too. As I drove, I looked at the buckle and thought about being at his home.

It had been a good season, even though we hadn't won the state tournament. No one had been kicked off the team for drinking or taking drugs. No one had failed to make his grades or been removed from the squad for disciplinary reasons. Nobody had impregnated one of the high school girls. We'd practiced hard and played hard and laughed together about a lot of things on the long bus rides over the winding roads of Arizona.

Throughout the past four months, I'd been told a number of times that my presence on the reservation would have a political impact on those living there. Maybe it would help them raise money for an economic or social cause. Maybe it would encourage minority cooperation with other ethnic groups or give them more clout in some of their future political fights. I hoped all those things happened, but the longer I stayed there, the more I felt that my experience with the tribe was not so much political as spiritual.

I was connected to the White Mountain Apache in the heart as well as the mind. I'd once had an historical appreciation of them as a people who had endured many hardships and survived, but that morning, as the miles rolled by and I moved away from the reservation, I had an appreciation of them as individuals trying to build their own lives each day, trying to mix the past with the present and create something new. This was an appreciation I would never have had if I hadn't gone there and worked with the kids and their coaches.

As the weeks had gone by this past winter, I had seen myself less as someone who was trying to change them or even help them; rather, I was simply getting to know them as human beings. And I was relearning the oldest lesson of all: Everything looks and feels differently when you stop viewing people from a distance and start interacting with them on a daily basis. That may be the only real cure for the ignorance and fear and prejudice that still pervade our world. The closer you get to others, the more you see that everyone is similar, yet everyone holds a different piece of the gift and mystery of life. It's our differences that make us stronger, not weaker.

I kept driving to the south and west, past the great forests on the reservation and the deep ravines that have been carved out of the earth over the millennia. I looked up at the red-faced mesas and the soaring hawks circling above them. The day was clear and the sky infinitely blue. I was going to miss this landscape and this great, clear light, but I knew I would come back soon.

The tribe had given me a seat on the board of the Apache Historical District, and I would return in April to help them make decisions about the restoration of Fort Apache and how to preserve other parts of their past. I would also return in May to see the largest graduating class ever at Alchesay High and the one with the largest number of students going on to college or military service. I would try to schedule another trip to Whiteriver the next fall, so I could visit the Falcons as they began their new basketball season. I wanted to see them practice and maybe give the big kids a few pointers on how to score in the paint.

My connection with the White Mountain Apache had been there for decades and was only growing deeper. It had probably been born in my childhood, when I began picking up arrowheads at the northern end of Manhattan and stuffing them into my pocket, feeling their rough edges as I walked around the city streets. I knew then, as I held those old weapons in my hand and imagined the battles that had been fought with them, that I was fascinated by history and wanted to delve more deeply into it.

I had been lucky enough to do that, getting to know some of America's indigenous people, who had been a part of our country's great and sometimes tragic past.

My connection with them would not end that day or the next week or in the near future. I had roots there now and I intended to nurture them and keep them alive. Who could ever say what tomorrow held? I might even be living permanently near the reservation someday.

Each time I fly over America and approach the Southwest, I look out the window and search the landscape for the Four Corners area, where the borders of Colorado, New Mexico, Arizona, and Utah all come together and form a cross. I glance to the south, down toward the land of the White Mountain Apache, and think about the Falcons. I think about building a house on my property in Colorado, and I think about making this my second home—about returning to the reservation and dropping in on the family whenever I feel like it.